12/02

To Aleta
+ Courtney

We hope you enjoy
the book

Tom + Theresa Rott

THE
JEWS IN AMERICA

David Cohen, Editor & Project Director
Mark Rykoff, Managing Editor
Jennifer Erwitt, General Manager
J. Curtis Sanburn, Chief Writer
Introduction by Chaim Potok

This book was made
possible with the generous assistance of
the Eastman Kodak Company

COLLINS PUBLISHERS

First Published in 1989 by Collins Publishers, Inc., San Francisco.
Copyright © 1989 by Collins Publishers, Inc.

ISBN 0-00-215323-8

Library of Congress Cataloging-in-Publication Data
Main entry under title: The Jews in America

1. Jews—United States—Pictorial works.
2. United States—Ethnic relations. I. Cohen, David, 1955-

E184.J5J656 1989
973'.04924 89-958

Printed in Japan   First printing June 1989

10   9   8   7 . 6   5   4   3   2   1

Cover: Photographed by Nick Kelsh in Milwaukee, WI
Page 4-5: Photographed by Genaro Molina in Sacramento, CA
Page 6-7: Photographed by Rick Rickman in Las Vegas, NV
Page 8-9: Photographed by Jim Mendenhall in Los Angeles, CA

Editor's Note

The Jews in America began with a simple idea. Then, like many creative enterprises, it took on a complex life of its own. The idea was to capture on film a cross section of the American Jewish community in all of its rich diversity—to photograph the daily life of a remarkable tribe that includes farmers and doctors, criminals, senators and Nobel Prize winners, black-suited Brooklyn *Lubavitchers* and pin-striped L.A. lawyers.

Our photographers spread out across the Jewish-American landscape to Squirrel Hill and Beverly Hills, Shaker Heights and Presidio Heights, Milwaukee, Kansas City, Great Neck and Maine. They came back with more than 2,000 rolls of film—photographs which were sometimes expected, often surprising and frequently moving.

Then it was left to the editors and designers to choose the best pictures and weave them into a convincing tapestry. This involved some tough decisions and close calls. Eighty thousand pictures were taken; only 200 or so could be used in the book. Great photographs and important subjects had to be left on the cutting room floor.

In preparing the text for this book, the writers and researchers had to decide which Hebrew and Yiddish terms to use and then how to spell and explain them. In most cases, we use modern Hebrew or Sephardic transliterations. Therefore, we refer to the Sabbath as *Shabbat*, rather than *Shabbes*, and the Feast of Tabernacles as *Sukkot*. There is an exception to this: When a term is most commonly known by its Yiddish name or Ashkenazic pronunciation, we use that. In other words, we don't call a *bris* a *brit*. We also wanted to make this book accessible to everyone. Therefore, each time we introduce a Hebrew or Yiddish term, we usually include a literal English translation.

We found during the course of this project—and we shouldn't have been surprised—that different people interpreted Jewish customs, traditions, rituals and even statistics in subtly and vastly different ways. We depended on a number of publications and modern-day Hillels to help us sort out these matters. Foremost among the books we used were the *1987-88 Jewish Almanac*, compiled and edited by Ivan L. Tillem; *The Jewish Book of Why* (vols. 1 & 2) by Alfred J. Kolatch; *Members of the Tribe: On the Road in Jewish America* by Ze'ev Chafets; and the *Code of Jewish Law* compiled by Rabbi Solomon Ganzfried, translated by Hyman E. Goldin. Biblical citations are from the 1917 translation published by the Jewish Publication Society of America.

Our panel of wise men and women included Rabbi Douglas Kahn of the San Francisco Jewish Community Relations Council, Dr. Jo Milgrom of the Center for Jewish Studies, Graduate Theological Union in Berkeley, John Rothmann, Rabbi Jacob Traub of Congregation Adath Israel in San Francisco and Rabbi Sheldon Waldenberg of Temple Isaiah in Lafayette, California. We are also are grateful to the many members of the Bay Area Jewish community who volunteered their time and creative energy, the editors of three dozen local Jewish newspapers who provided us with valuable information; and of course, the Jewish families across America who welcomed photographers into their homes.

Finally, I want to mention an 85-year-old woman named Ida Brody Mintz. She came to America from Vilna, Lithuania, at age 13 speaking only Yiddish. She somehow managed to put herself through law school and her brother through medical school. Observing ancient traditions over seven decades of mind-boggling change, she has led a happy and productive life as a Jew in America. Even now, she belongs to a wide array of charitable organizations and study groups. My grandmother's life here is most remarkable because it is not unique. Most Jews in America can tell a similar family story—and as they tell it, they usually feel exceptionally lucky that they were born in such a place and time.

—David Cohen

Hear, O Israel: The Lord our God, the Lord is One. And thou shalt love the Lord thy God with all thy heart, and with all thy soul, and with all thy might.

And these words, which I command thee this day, shall be upon thy heart; and thou shalt teach them diligently to thy children …

and shalt talk of them when thou sittest in thy house, and when thou walkest by the way, and when thou liest down, and when thou risest up.—Deuteronomy 6:4-7

Introduction

"To collect photographs is to collect the world," writes Susan Sontag in her book *On Photography*. We open this book and pass into a wondrous world of pictures that offers us not only an excursion into the exquisite landscape of sophisticated modern photography but also the opportunity to pause, gaze and reflect upon what has been wrought in this country by Jews in only four generations.

One needs to know how to "read" these pictures in order to understand that this volume is in essence a discerning essay on the current condition of America's Jews: their triumphant and unprecedented integration into the host culture since their mass beginning on these shores in the 1880s and the sobering problems this success has brought about.

Long threads bind these images to the past. The young men who hold *Torah* scrolls and read from them; the scribe and his family gathered around a large scroll of parchment; the child with a *Simhat Torah* flag; the men who joyously carry their new *Torah* beneath a *hupah*—all have their origins in the Jewish people's passion for the Covenant. Embodied by the sacred scrolls, this Covenant is the central concept that has propelled the Jewish people through history. It is the indissoluble contract with God or destiny, that still profoundly awesome and mysterious relationship between the Jew and the world.

There are pictures of people lighting *Hanukkah* candles, dwelling in the *sukkah*, participating in the Sabbath meal and the Passover *Seder*. The contemporary picture of a young man laying *tefillin* in his university dorm room surrounded by posters and images from the popular culture brings to mind another photograph I once saw of an old immigrant Jew celebrating the Sabbath in a tenement cellar dark and dense with coal bins. He had spread a white cloth on a small table before sitting down to his sacred meal. All around him shimmered a nimbus of white light; beyond him was the grimy world he left behind as he entered the realm of the Covenant. Both are images of the way Jews give the covenantal relationship tangible expression: links between man and God.

The many multi-generational images—grandparents, parents, children, grandchildren—depict another covenant: links between man and man. The family has always been the sacred unit of the Jewish people, its building block. Preserve that unit and you preserve the people. A cluster of families forms a community; and a dedicated community, one that respects and cares for all life, from youth to advanced age, is the goal and the gift of the Covenant people. Hence, the images in these pages of the young and the old in various communal activities.

For the American Jew today, that forging of a just and caring community often involves social action, public service, commitment to law or medicine, a passion for science or the arts. Consciously or unconsciously, American Jews continue to view the devout medieval doctor of law and medicine, Moses Maimonides, and the modern physicist and humanist, Albert Einstein, as paradigms for contemporary Jewry.

Not only professionals and intellectuals gaze at us from between these covers. There are hardhats here as well, cowboys, manual laborers, storekeepers, people who work long and hard with their hands. I look at them and am frequently reminded of the simple people of Eastern European Jewry—wagon-drivers, water-carriers, wood-choppers, textile workers, dairymen, farmers— the laboring masses.

But there is one overriding difference between that old Jewish world and the new Jewish American world. Never before have Jews participated in the core of the host culture. No matter what contributions were made in the past by Jews to the societies in which they lived, it was never possible for them to affect the essential nature of those societies. The situation is altogether different today: Jews are part of the very substance of American civilization. In that lies enormous opportunity and significant risk. Some of that risk is shown in this book: the disintegration of core Jewish values; the splintering of the Jewish community into dissident factions; even the previously unthinkable prevalence among Jews of alcoholism and drug abuse.

Two dynamics are occurring simultaneously among America's six million Jews: continuing and, in many instances, increasing commitments to Jewish concerns (religious education, Israel, Soviet Jewry) by about two-thirds of the group, and flight from virtually all things Jewish by the rest. Will the committed two-thirds succeed in fashioning an authentic American-Jewish civilization, one rich in new forms of individual and communal expression—as did the Jews of Babylonia, who, two thousand years ago, created a host of new Jewish institutions along with the Babylonian talmud? Or will American Jewry become a modern-day version of the vanished, culturally attenuated Jewry of ancient Alexandria—so much a part of their culture that they finally faded into it?

The future is hidden; the jury, still out. Meanwhile, we have the remarkable images in this book as clear evidence of the present concerns, preoccupations, vitality and vulnerability of the Jews in America.

— Chaim Potok

Bris: Eight days after he is born, a Jewish boy makes acquaintance with one of Judaism's most venerable institutions: the *mohel*. Technically, any competent Jew can be a *mohel*, the one who circumcises infant boys, but a good *mohel* is usually a specialist who has mastered a swift and delicate art.

The circumcision ceremony is called *bris*, meaning covenant. In Genesis 17:11, God promises to bless Abraham and all of his children if he, in turn, will be loyal to God. Their covenant is sealed with a sign that cannot be hidden: "Circumcise the flesh of your foreskin, and that shall be the mark of the Covenant between you and Me." Four thousand years later, the *bris* remains one of the oldest consistently observed rituals known to humanity.

Photographed by Shelley Kusnetz in Millburn, NJ

Left: Apprehension. The family and friends of David and Ryna Alexander gather in the living room to witness the *bris* of Sam Raphael Alexander, born September 29, 1988.
Photographed by Nick Kelsh in Cherry Hill, NJ

Below: Relief. Joel Shoulson, an eighth-generation *mohel*, performs about 20 ritual circumcisions per week. Based in Philadelphia, he and his father developed state-of-the-art circumcision instruments now used in hospitals around the world. After the *bris*, Joel comforts 8-day-old Nathaniel Martin Maxwell Goldman. First-time parents Robert Goldman and Susannah Maxwell and grandfather Leonard Goldman look on.
Photographed by Nick Kelsh in Wilmington, DE

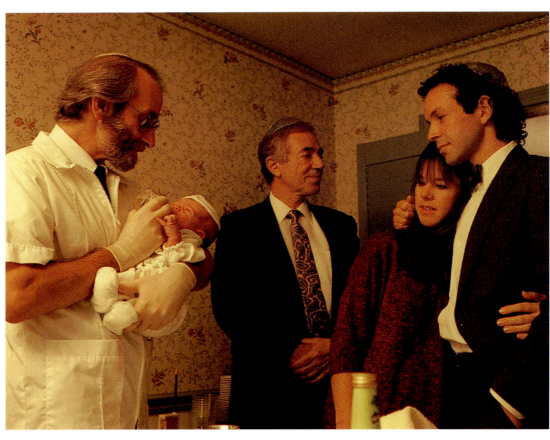

Left: A generational *tableau vivant*. On Thanksgiving Day, the women of the Fineman family adore 2-month-old Maxim Ernst Alexander Ludwig, the first member of the next generation. Max is the son of Dana Fineman (lower left) and her German husband, Gerd Ludwig. Clockwise from top left: great-grandmother Mary "Mimi" Fineman, grandmother Sande Fineman, great-grandmother Sylvia Kessler and Aunt Karen Fineman. Mimi calls Max "the joy of my life—named after my late husband." Says Sylvia, "I have eight grandchildren, but to have a great-grandchild is a wonderful dividend."
Photographed by Douglas Kirkland in Beverly Hills, CA

Below: Gabriel Vaenberg shows a little brotherly love toward his 2-month-old sister, Alexandra. The children's father is from Argentina and mom is from St. Louis. The kids are being raised bilingually.
Photographed by Patrick Tehan in St. Louis, MO

Above: Eight-month-old Rachel Friedman watches the *Simhat Torah* festivities at Wilshire Boulevard Temple. Jewish congregations read portions of the *Torah* (the five Books of Moses) each Sabbath in an annual cycle. On *Simhat Torah* (rejoicing in the *Torah*) they complete the last two verses of Deuteronomy and begin the cycle again with the first verses of Genesis.
Photographed by Elaine Isaacson in Los Angeles, CA

Left: The Katz family of Brooklyn vacations at the Arlington Hotel in the White Mountains of New Hampshire. Here, Jonathan Katz, 27, reads to 16-month-old Rachel while 2-year-old Shalom *kibitzes* from the window.
Photographed by Stephen Muskie in Bethlehem, NH

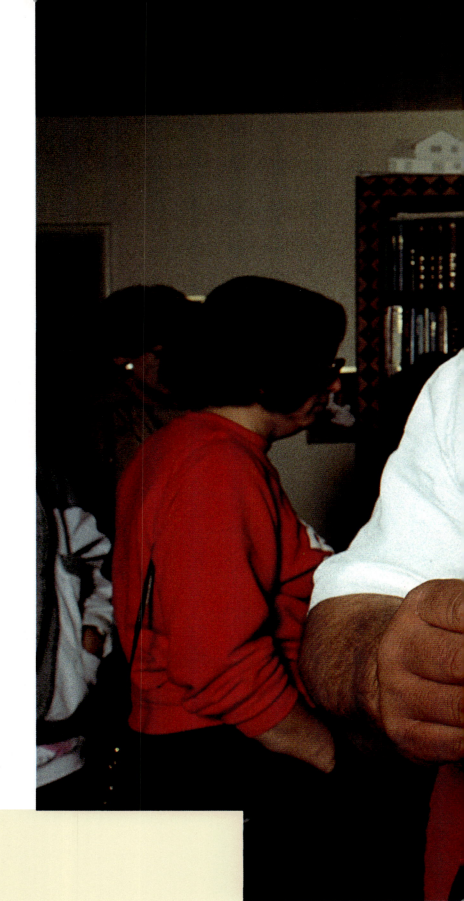

O*psherenish*: Until the age of 3, many Orthodox boys are allowed to grow uncut manes of hair. The *opsherenish*, or ritual first haircut, often takes place on the holiday of *Lag B'Omer* when the boy's father invites friends and family to each cut off a small lock. Above, a slightly disconcerted Yanky Richler holds still while his grandfather, Scholom Raskin, cuts one of the few remaining locks. Usually, a professional barber finishes up the job, leaving only the *peyot* (sidelocks) unshorn.

Photographed by Elaine Isaacson in Long Beach, CA

Above: On the afternoon of the first day of *Rosh Hashanah* (the two-day Jewish New Year observance), worshipers in Brooklyn gather to perform the ritual of *tashlikh*. After reading prayers, they will cast crumbs from their pockets into a body of water—in this case a fountain just out of camera range. The custom is based on a reading of Micah 7:19, "And Thou wilt cast all their sins into the depths of the sea."
Photographed by Steve Krongard in Brooklyn, NY

Right: Rabbi Mark Miller of Temple Bat Yahm marks the arrival of the High Holy Days with the wail of the *shofar*, one of the oldest wind instruments in the world. The *shofar* is fashioned from a ram's horn to commemorate Abraham's sacrifice of a lamb in place of his son Isaac. According to Genesis, this occurred on *Rosh Hashanah*, the first day of the month of *Tishri*. In Biblical days, the *shofar* frightened the enemy, announced war and called the people to assembly. When Israeli troops took control of the Old City of Jerusalem during the Six-Day War of 1967, the *shofar* sounded their victory.
Photographed by Elaine Isaacson in Newport Beach, CA

Left: Donald and Joan Green tear the *hallah* (braided bread) at a *Yom Kippur* break-fast at the home of their close friends, the Levisons. On *Yom Kippur*, the Day of Atonement, Jews fast from sunset until the stars appear 25 hours later. In this manner, they wash themselves of their sins and start the New Year with a clean slate.

Below: Wearing a bright *yarmulka* and *tallit* he made as a teen-ager in summer camp, Mark Green Solomons, 27, makes *havdalah* (the ceremony marking the end of a festival) at the Levison's *Yom Kippur* break-fast. Among Mark's fancy *mishpahah* are his grandmother, Edie Green, a rare fourth-generation San Franciscan—and Rabbi Gershom Mendes Seixas, one of the clergymen who administered the presidential oath of office to George Washington in 1789.
Photographed by Doug Menuez in San Francisco, CA

Ye shall dwell in booths seven days ... that your generations may know that I made the children of Israel to dwell in booths when I brought them out of the land of Egypt.—Leviticus 23:42-43.

The holiday of *Sukkot* has two distinct origins. In pre-Biblical times, *Sukkot* was a harvest festival named after the temporary booths or huts built to shelter workers in the fields. Similar huts provided shelter for the Israelites during their 40-year flight from Egypt. Today, by re-creating the flimsy, hastily constructed *sukkah*, modern Jews both celebrate God's bounty and commemorate His special concern for the Children of Israel when He led them through a perilous wilderness.

While few people spend a full week in the airy, branch-covered huts, many families decorate them, have meals in them and, on clear fall nights, camp out in them to relive the star-lit hopes and fears of a people on its way to the Promised Land.

Left: Rick Schwag, executive director of the Jewish Living and Learning Network, covers the roof of his Vermont *sukkah* with branches, and hangs small pumpkins and squash from the beams. Tradition requires that stars must be able to shine down on those inside. This *sukkah* will be the focus of an October *Sukkot* retreat for about 20 New Englanders. **Photographed by Jim Estrin in Lyndonville, VT**

Below: Michael Omer-Man decorates a *sukkah* in his backyard.
Photographed by Bill Aron in Los Angeles, CA

Following page: The Brown family *sukkah*. Seated around the temporary dining table are Steve and Michele Brown and their children, Dory and Aliza.
Photographed by Nick Kelsh in Melrose Park, PA

Train up a child in the way he should go, and even when he is old, he will not depart from it.—Proverbs 22:6

Left: Third-graders at Congregation Ner Tamid approach the altar during *Tot Shabbat*, a special Sabbath service for youngsters. The theme for this *Tot Shabbat* is Noah's ark, and the kids are excited because the local Humane Society has promised to bring live animals.
Photographed by Rick Rickman in Las Vegas, NV

Below: On Thursdays, the Perl children make *hallah* for *Shabbat* (Sabbath). Once they finish getting the dough all over the place, they'll collect it again and braid it into two loaves.
Photographed by Ricardo DeAratanha in Los Angeles, CA

Preceding page photographed by Bradley Clift in Bloomfield, CT

Photographed by Bradley Clift in Bloomfield, CT

Photographed by Skeeter Hagler in Bay City, TX

Photographed by Jerry Valente in New York City, NY

Photographed by Richard Marshall in Chicago, IL

Who finds a faithful friend finds a treasure.—Ben Sira 6:14

Left: Esti Lax, age 7, and Rivky Traxler, age 9, are best friends who live across the street from each other in the heavily Jewish Fondren section of Houston. "Sometimes we help each other out," Rivky says. "I give her things that are my own, my own special things that I won't give to anybody else."
Photographed by Skeeter Hagler in Houston, TX

Above: Dancing partners Emily Brach and Julia Weiner warm up for ballet class, held every Wednesday at the United Synagogue of Greater Hartford.
Photographed by Bradley Clift in Hartford, CT.

Left: The Milwaukee Jewish Day School has grown steadily since its inception in 1981. "There's a renewed interest among parents to establish a stronger Jewish identity for their children," says school director Doris Shneidman.
Photographed by Nick Kelsh in Milwaukee, WI

Above: *Hassidic* school children smile at Ernesto Bazan's camera just before the photographer was shooed away by angry teachers. In late-20th-century America, few neighborhoods are as resolutely 18th-century European as Brooklyn's Williamsburg section, home to the *Satmar Hassidim*. Fiercely isolationist and ultra-Orthodox, the *Satmar* shun many aspects of contemporary American life. A generation ago, there were 30,000 *Satmar* and *Lubavitcher Hassidim* in Brooklyn. Today, mostly through natural increase, the population has more than doubled.
Photographed by Ernesto Bazan in Brooklyn, NY

Above: Stephen Goldmeier is "a basic, ordinary, regular kid," his father, David, explains. Stephen gets up early on Sunday mornings to go with his dad and brother and sister to services, breakfast and Sunday school at Beth Jacob Synagogue.
Photographed by Randy Olson in Columbus, OH

Right: At Oholei Torah school, a *Hassidic yeshiva* (religious academy) in Brooklyn, the youngsters study *Torah* in the mornings and history, science and math in the afternoons. The *yeshiva* has played a central role in Jewish life ever since the destruction of the Second Temple in Jerusalem in 70 C.E. Under the leadership of Rabbi Yohanan ben Zakkai, Jewish scholars who fled Jerusalem reassembled and created the first central *yeshiva* in a small town called Yavneh near present-day Tel Aviv. From Yavneh to Babylonia to Toledo in Spain to Vilna in Lithuania and, following the Holocaust, to America, the *yeshiva* has maintained the lifeblood of Jewish scholarship around the world.
Photographed by Jerry Valente in Brooklyn, NY

Left: Two days before the Day of Atonement, inside the Lubavitch World Headquarters in Brooklyn, Aaron Ceitlin teaches his 6-year-old son, Menachem, some fine points of prayer.
Photographed by Jerry Valente in Brooklyn, NY

Above: "Temple should be relevant to everyone," says Rabbi Donald Weber of Temple Rodeph Torah. At the once-a-month Very Young People's *Shabbat*, Brett Willner, and Rabbi Weber's sons, Ariel and Noah, enjoy the song, "Bim Bam."
Photographed by April Saul in Marlboro, NJ

Right: After *Shabbat* dinner, Annie Busis, left, wins a game of hide-and-seek in the coat room of Squirrel Hill's new Jewish Community Center.
Photographed by Melissa Farlow in Pittsburgh, PA

Below: Every *Shabbat*, Stanley Weinstein takes his 11-year-old son, Moshe, to services at Lake Park Synagogue in Milwaukee. In 1983, several young Jewish families, most of whom had become observant only recently, formed the congregation, the first new Orthodox synagogue in Milwaukee in more than 40 years.
Photographed by Nick Kelsh in Milwaukee, WI

Be bold as a leopard, light as an eagle, swift as a deer and mighty as a lion to do the will of the Father in Heaven.—Mishnah: Pirke Avot 5:20

Right: Brant Lake Camp has won the Adirondack Invitational Swim Meet nearly every year since 1978. Founded in 1916, the camp has been owned and operated by the same family for three generations. Campers Marc Shalam, 11 (nearest), and Jeff Schachter, 12 (second from left), both from Old Westbury, New York, give it everything they've got to keep up BLC's winning tradition.
Photographed by Jochen Manz in Brant Lake, NY

Below: Every summer, 300 kids from the New York metropolitan area travel north to Camp Monroe in the Hudson River Valley for eight weeks of swimming, playing kickball, feeding the goats and ducks, singing Yiddish and Hebrew folk songs and keeping *kosher* (following the dietary laws). The kids' parents pay $3,300 per child for the eight-week session, a price that is considered mid-range for New York-area summer camps. Left to right: (first row) Jennifer Krieger, Erica Siegel, Stephanie Hertz, Fraidy Felsinger, Emily Amdurer and (top row) Sharry Braunstein and Jessica Ganz head to the lake for a swim.
Photographed by camp director Stanley Felsinger in Monroe, NY

Preceding page photographed by Nathan Benn in Brooklyn, NY

… whoever brings up an orphan in his home, Scripture ascribes it to him as though he had begotten him.—Talmud: Sanhedrin 19b

Left: Brian Goldfarb is one of three foster children living in Hilda Arshenovitz's suburban Cleveland home. Hilda has played mother to more than 70 emotionally disturbed children over the past 34 years. "I originally planned to do it for a year," she says, "but there was always another child who needed me." Of Brian, Hilda says, "He's very bright, he's fun, and he likes to be helpful. Tonight, he set the *Shabbat* table with my grandson. Living with a family has meant a great deal to him."
Photographed by Randy Olson in Cleveland, OH

Below: Ilene Tanen describes her 13-year-old son Ben, as a great kid and a wonderful student. "He's interested in everything," she says brightly. Ben keeps an extensive and immaculate stamp collection; competes in baseball, basketball and runs cross-country; plays clarinet in the school band; and is active in the Temple Sinai youth group. Ilene's one concern: "He's getting to be very adolescent," she says. "He likes to torment his sisters a little bit."
Photographed by Peter Essick in Roslyn, NY

Left: But seriously, folks. Four-year-old Ira Scher and his mother, Elaine, enjoy the *Tot Shabbat* services at Congregation Ner Tamid in Las Vegas.
Photographed by Rick Rickman in Las Vegas, NV

Above: "You know, you live life and you give birth, and then one of your children turns out to be Steven Spielberg!" exclaims Leah Adler, Spielberg's mother and owner of "The Milky Way," a *kosher* restaurant in L.A. The first of four children, Spielberg has directed and/or produced seven of the top 20 money-making films of all time, including *Jaws, Close Encounters of the Third Kind, E.T.* and *Raiders of the Lost Ark*.
Photographed by Brian Lanker in Los Angeles, CA

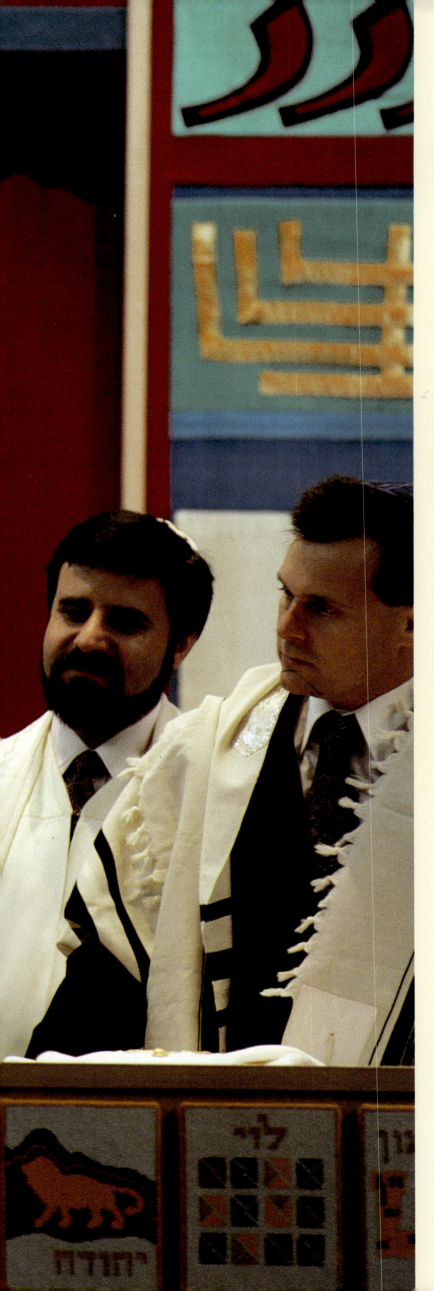

Bar Mitzvah: A boy becomes a *Bar Mitzvah* (Son of the Commandment) upon reaching the age of 13, at which time he acquires adult status. In the religious community, this means he is counted in the *minyan*, the quorum for public prayer. It also means that he is accountable for his own conduct. Thus, it is traditional at the *Bar Mitzvah* ceremony for the father to publicly bless God, "who has relieved me of this one's responsibility." *Bar Mitzvah* status also allows the boy to be called to bless the *Torah*. In honor of this event, he is usually prepared to chant from the *Torah* and from the appropriate prophetic portion (*Haftorah*) that accompanies the *Torah* reading.

Some boys need a crash course in Hebrew to read their *Torah* and *Haftorah*. Ari Lit, left, however, attended private Hebrew school from third to sixth grade, so reading and understanding Hebrew posed little problem. Ari felt confident as he stepped onto the *bimah* (platform) at Congregation Brith Shalom in Houston. But, predictably, when he saw all his friends and relatives in the congregation, confidence deserted him—momentarily at least.

For Ari, the *Bar Mitzvah* ceremony signified that he is no longer a child. "I feel that I have to be more mature and responsible," he says. "Now I do my homework and my parents don't have to bug me first. And when I go to *shul* (synagogue) and put on a *tallit*, I feel like another man there, not a boy."

Below: Ari guides his reading in the *Torah* with a silver pointer called a *yad*, which in Hebrew simply means "hand." The *yad* is used to show proper respect for Judaism's holiest object, to keep the handwritten parchment clean and to keep one's place.

Ari Lit's *Bar Mitzvah* was photographed by Shelly Katz in Houston, TX

Left: The men important to Ari's passage into manhood join him at the *bimah*. From left: Ari's father Mark Lit, his grandfather Joseph Lit and Rabbi Shaul Osadchey.

Above: About 50 of Ari's relatives flew in from the East Coast to celebrate his *Bar Mitzvah*. Ari and his cousin, Leah Silverman, dance cheek-to-cheek at the reception.

Recognizing the growing emancipation of women, Reconstructionist Jewish congregations introduced the *Bat Mitzvah* ceremony in America in the early 1920s. Nowadays, nearly all Conservative and Reform congregations, as well as some Orthodox, hold this female rite of passage. Some congregations account for the earlier maturation of girls and hold *Bat Mitzvahs* on the girl's 12th birthday.

Left: As part of Marci Haas' *Bat Mitzvah* ceremony, she and her mother, Sharon, listen as older sister Nicole recites the *havdalah*, the service that separates *Shabbat* from the rest of the week.

Below: Nicole gives Marci some make-up tips on the morning of her *Bat Mitzvah* ceremony.
Photographed by Randy Olson in Cincinnati, OH

Bar and Bat Mitzvah parties photographed by Mary Ellen Mark in Alpine and Asbury Park, NJ

I t's a wedding of sorts, the marriage of a congregation to its new *Torah*. In Sacramento, Rabbi Stuart Rosen carries a newly inscribed *Sefer Torah* under a makeshift *hupah* (canopy). He leads about 100 members of the Knesset Israel Torah Center out of the synagogue and into the sunshine. Singing and dancing, the festive parade trips down Morse Avenue, past curious onlookers and a tag football game.

Preparing a new *Torah* can take 2,000 hours. The five Books of Moses are handwritten in Hebrew on parchment, using a turkey quill and an elaborate calligraphy to form the scroll's 304,805 letters. Although most of the work on this *Torah* was done in Israel, the final 500 letters were inscribed on behalf of the congregation by Rabbi Shimon Kraft of Los Angeles.

Photographed by Genaro Molina in Sacramento, CA

Preceding page: The Kase family of Great Neck, Long Island, was kind (and brave) enough to allow photographer Nina Barnett to infiltrate their home for nearly a week. Nina returned the favor in typical photojournalist's fashion by photographing the family in less-than-formal situations.

Sunday morning in the Kase household almost always includes the Sunday *New York Times*. Clockwise around the bed, starting with dad: John Kase, a lawyer in Garden City and an electronics buff; Marjorie, a seventh-grader, "always has her nose in a book"; Elizabeth, an eleventh-grader, "always out of the house"; and last but not least, Arlene, a speech therapist with the Rockville Centré Public Schools.

Left: "My room's usually like this. It's homey and everything is right where I can reach it," says Marjorie, who attends Great Neck North Middle School.

Below: Who has time for math? Elizabeth and her boyfriend, Idan Elkon, 17, have been dating for more than a year and often do homework together in the Kase's family room. Idan qualifies as a dream boyfriend: First, he's a senior at Great Neck North High School, where Elizabeth is a junior. Second, he's a major jock—all-Nassau County hockey player and star first-baseman on the baseball team. Third, he's cute.

The Kase family was photographed by Nina Barnett in Great Neck, NY

Left: In his dorm room, Reuben Beiser, a sophomore at Brown University, dons *tallit* and *tefillin* (phylacteries) for morning prayers. Reuben lives in Hebrew House, a co-ed section of his dormitory organized by and for Orthodox and Conservative Jews who wish to keep *kosher* and reinforce their sense of Jewish community. "In America," Reuben says, "the emphasis on individuality allows most Jewish communities to ignore questions of identity. Here in Hebrew House, I try to reaffirm my identity every day."

After graduation, this Rhode Island native plans to return to a *yeshiva* in Israel, where he had studied for two years prior to college. "The future of Judaism lies in Israel," Reuben says excitedly, "and that is where I feel most fulfilled."
Photographed by Bill Ballenberg in Providence, RI

Below: #0836: *Your mother will love me! Romantic, caring, nice Jewish girl, looking for a romantic mensch.* #0834: *If champagne is your flair, good conversation, gourmet dining and dancing in the moonlight, I am your man.* #0078: *Good looking sexy blonde with 3rd-degree black belt in shopping needs handsome guy with gold card.* #0309: *A female who would never think of writing a personal seeking a tall, professional male who would never think of answering one.* #0261: *Great looking guy must get married or will lose custody of cat—judge requires stable home life.*

—A selection of entries from the Concord Resort Hotel's *Meeter's Digest,* a compendium of personal ads placed by some of the 2,000 guests who registered for the famous Catskill inn's semi-annual Singles Weekend.
Photographed by Misha Erwitt in Kiamesha Lake, NY

Left: "Most single people don't like traditional singles scenes," says Patti Breitman, group leader of the Bay Area Jewish Singles Hiking Club. "The beauty of our club is that people who love hiking know that they will meet other hikers. In fact, at least two married couples that I know of met on one of our trips."
Photographed by Doug Menuez on Mt. Tamalpais in Marin County, CA

Above: "I hadn't known many Jewish people before I met Brian," says Marilyn Zabczyk, 22, about her fiancé, Brian Fishel, 23. When Brian proposed marriage, Marilyn, raised as a Roman Catholic, decided she wanted to know more about Judaism. Together, the couple took a course called "Introduction to Judaism" at Hebrew Union College in Cincinnati.

"During the course, I decided to convert," Marilyn says. "Brian and I had talked about it; talked about what we wanted out of life, and about how we wanted to raise our family. We wanted a firm religious base in our home. I decided that Judaism was right for me. Why? It was just a feeling I got when we went to services together ... the emphasis on family. Judaism is a liveable religion. It changes yet stays the same for centuries."

Marilyn was shepherded through her conversion study by Rabbi Lewis Kamrass of the Isaac M. Wise Temple in Cincinnati. With Kamrass standing at the lectern, the happy couple embrace after the conversion ceremony. "Yes, I am Jewish," Marilyn affirms.
Photographed by Randy Olson in Cincinnati, OH

On October 23, 1988, Karen Shechter, an accountant, and Mitchell Stern, a business executive, were married at Congregation B'nai Amoona in St. Louis. Both in their late 20s, Karen and Mitchell fell in love through a conspiracy hatched by mutual friends. "I was ready to get married," Karen says, "and I knew Mitchell was the right person."

Karen is the sixth generation of her family to belong to the Conservative B'nai Amoona congregation. Mitchell, who grew up in a Reform household, says he will join B'nai Amoona, as Karen's father did when he married her mother. The newlyweds say they plan to keep *kosher* eventually, but for now they do not. According to Karen, "In a marriage, there's give and take, and not keeping *kosher* from the start was, for me, a give."

At right, Karen's father fixes her veil just before the walk down the aisle. Immediately after the ceremony, the groom will smash a wine glass with his foot. The explanations for this custom are numerous: an expression of remembrance for the destruction of the Temple in Jerusalem in 70 C.E.; a loud noise to scare off evil spirits. But most likely it is just a reminder of the deeply held Jewish conviction that life's most joyous moments must be tempered in order to forestall misfortune.

The Shechter-Stern wedding was photographed by Patrick Tehan in St. Louis, MO

Left: Mitchell, Karen, her aunt Blanche Horwitz and sister Sharon Rosen pose for the official wedding photographer after the ceremony.

Above: Under a shower of pink, heart-shaped confetti, in the strong arms of her husband, Karen is carried away from her wedding banquet at the St. Louis Marriott ("The best *kosher* service in St. Louis," says Barbara Shechter, mother of the bride). Then it's on to Mexico for the honeymoon.

Left: At the wedding reception, Harry Shechter, the happy father of the bride, swings off his daughter and onto the arm of his wife, Barbara.
Photographed by Patrick Tehan in St. Louis, MO

Above and below: Sephardic Temple Tifereth Israel is "the most beautiful synagogue in Los Angeles," according to bride Wendy Kamenoff. Wendy and her new husband, Steve Mittleman, kiss under the *hupah* after the wedding vows. In ages past, the *hupah* was a private tent for "marital union." Since then, through centuries of evolving custom, the *hupah* has become simply the public canopy under which a Jewish bride and groom are married.

Mutual friends introduced Mittleman and Kamenoff when Steve was in New York to play a role in Woody Allen's film *Radio Days*. A long-distance romance followed. "We wrote a lot of very romantic letters and talked on the phone every day for an hour," recalls Wendy. Finally, after nearly two years, Wendy moved to Los Angeles and the couple married.
Photographed by Jim Mendenhall in Los Angeles, CA

Above: Completely unfurled, the Gerstle-Sloss family tree spreads 15 feet across the living room floor of the Levison home in San Francisco. The tree contains more than 500 names and dates back to 1740. Family reunions take place in Marin County's Gerstle Park every seven years or so and usually include about 200 people. As older generations pass, their sons and daughters assume the mantle, organizing reunions and maintaining the tree. Here Peter Levison reviews family connections with daughter Beth (to his left), sister Elinor Gross and her son Matthew and husband, David.
Photographed by Doug Menuez in San Francisco, CA

Right: Matthew Gross, a fifth-generation Californian, studies portraits of his ancestors in a book about the Gerstle and Sloss families. Lewis Gerstle and Louis Sloss, both originally from Germany, immigrated to Sacramento during the Gold Rush to sell provisions to miners. In the 1850s, they each married a Greenbaum sister and started two distinguished California families. Matthew's mother, Elinor Gross, and his uncle, Peter Levison, join him in the Levison living room to recount ancestral exploits in the Old West.

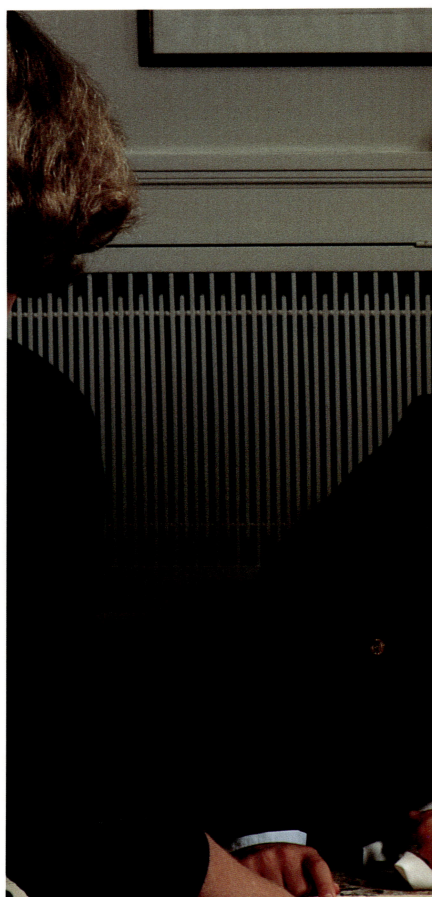

Above: "They pout a hundred times a day," Dane Kostin says. "There's always something going on in our household ... you never know what's afoot." At the breakfast room table, Dane has a tête-á-tête with youngest daughter, Jessie, age four.

Right: They met in law school at Boston University. Seventeen years later, Dane is managing partner of a 60-lawyer firm in suburban Hartford, while his wife, Michele, practices real-estate law, managing a staff of 16 lawyers for Aetna Life & Casualty.

In his precious free time, Dane is chairman of the board of the Bess & Paul Sigel Hebrew Academy, where the three older Kostin children attend school. Splendidly dressed for the Academy's annual scholarship dinner, Michele and Dane pose for the camera on their way out the door.

Below: Michele says her 6-year-old daughter, Elisabeth, is a "deep, sensitive, private person. She takes things seriously." A first-grader at the Hebrew Academy, Elisabeth already knows enough Hebrew to have been given her own prayer book, a *siddur*. "The school made a party of it," Michele says. "Little things like that become big events in our lives."

Despite the tough times, Mark Khromchenko is happy to be here. "America is a great, big country," he says. "I like America because it is a free country. I feel freedom for myself."

In his hometown of Odessa in the Soviet Union, Khromchenko was a duly recognized and rewarded structural engineer. Still, he and his wife, Alla, decided to emigrate to the United States in the fall of 1988, taking their young son, Elijah, and Khromchenko's mother, father, sister and niece with them.

The Khromchenkos left behind pervasive anti-Semitism and a hopeless economy that stirred vivid dreams of freedom. They also left behind guaranteed housing, guaranteed work—and all that was familiar. Upon arrival in America, their new-found freedom took on a sober aspect when they came face-to-face with the fact that employment had to be found and kept; housing had to be found and paid for.

To help the Khromchenkos and the thousands of Soviet Jews who have come to the United States, the American Jewish community has put together one of the best, most comprehensive support networks for immigrants in the history of private benefaction. Through the New York Association for New Americans (NYANA) and the Jewish Community House (JCH), the Khromchenkos receive crucial financial aid, English language education, vocational training, job-placement assistance, red-tape counseling, and a 10th-floor, two-bedroom apartment in the heart of Brooklyn's Russian-Jewish immigrant community.

Still, Khromchenko must find a job. At the moment, his English is not good enough to handle the technical jargon used in engineering. He says he'll take whatever employment he can get. So he studies and sends carefully composed résumés out by the dozen. He knows his future, as bright as it may be, is no longer guaranteed.

The Khromchenko family was photographed by Andy Levin in Brooklyn, NY

Above: At home, Mark Khromchenko tickles his 3-year-old-son, Elijah.

Right: Victor Khromchenko, Mark's father, is studying English like his son. He helps with the grand-children, does a lot of the family's shopping with his wife, Polina, and enjoys a little TV now and then.

Below: Mark's niece, Tania, has been doing excep-tionally well in school since her arrival in the United States. A ninth-grader at Franklin Delano Roosevelt High School, she gets the highest possible grades in all her subjects, including English as a Second Language. In her free time, four times each week, Tania tutors a younger neighborhood girl in English.

Left: Kenneth Gordon's great-grandfather was a tailor in Russia and his grandfather made women's clothes in New York. His father sold shirts wholesale, and Kenneth sold neckwear in Cleveland before opening Kenneth Gordon New Orleans in 1975. Now, the company produces a complete line of men's and women's clothing, which it sells under its own and private labels.

Three generations of Gordons pose for a family portrait. From right: Kenneth, chairman and chief executive officer; Helen, treasurer; and son, Joel, assistant manager in the shirt factory cutting department.

Above: Kenneth's mother, Helen, also comes from a family of tailors. "She has a knack for finding things that aren't running smoothly," says Kenneth. How does Kenneth like running a business full of family? "Wonderful!" he exclaims. "There is no greater pleasure in life than sharing with family, and not just the happiness, the woes, too."
Photographed by Patrick Tehan in New Orleans, LA

Above: The Denn brothers—Manuel, Herman and Sidney—started merchandising right after World War II. As young vets, fresh from stations in Japan, Germany and Hawaii, they came home to Texas and bought up $1,500 worth of GI surplus which they promptly resold. By 1949 the wartime surplus had dried up, and the brothers opened a sporting goods store selling team-sport supplies and hunting and fishing gear. Today, Denn Brothers Sporting Goods in Bay City, Texas, (population 18,000) does close to $1 million in sales each year. Nevertheless, Sidney figures he and his brothers will eventually have to sell their 40-year-old family enterprise; the next generation of Denns have all resettled elsewhere, from Houston to Los Angeles to Tel Aviv.
Photographed by Skeeter Hagler in Bay City, TX

Right: Trimmings, Velcro, thread, buttons, zippers, ribbons, notions. Even today, dry goods shops sprout like mushrooms on the Lower East Side of New York.
Photographed by Andy Levin in New York City, NY

Tenement buildings on Orchard Street in the heart of Manhattan's Lower East Side stand as living monuments to the history of the Jews in America. By 1900, the second major wave of Jewish immigration had landed more than a half-million very poor Eastern European Jews in New York. Most of them found their way to the Lower East Side and the infamous Tenth Ward, which became the most fiercely congested ghetto in America, perhaps in the world. Some blocks had population densities as high as 700 per acre.

Struggling to gain a foothold in this bewildering new world, the new arrivals worked 70 hours a week in the sweatshops of the garment industry or set off on their own as peddlers. The religious broke *Shabbat* laws and worked in order to eat; they watched their children, schooled on the streets, grow harsh and disrespectful. It was a difficult time in a place that stirred burning homesickness for the green hills of Vilna or the pauperish gentility of the *shtetl*.

But the average stay of Jewish immigrants in the Lower East Side was only 15 years. They moved on—and up—first to Harlem, then to the Bronx and Brooklyn and then across America. Today, only about 30,000 Jews live here—shopkeepers, blue-collar workers, Hebraists, rabbis, teachers and social workers. They live side by side with Chinese, Blacks, Hispanics and yuppies. On Sundays, the Lower East Side is jammed with shoppers, often uptown and suburban Jews, who come back to the earthy street bazaars on Orchard and Canal streets looking for bargains.

Photographed by Steve Krongard in New York City, NY

Below: The Jewish attorneys at Wyman, Bautzer, Kuchel & Silbert,
a general-practice firm in Century City, gather for a group photo.
Photographed by Bill Aron in Los Angeles, CA

Above: In 1977, the law firm of Hurwitz & Fine in Buffalo started with two partners and two associates. Today, the firm numbers 20 attorneys working in various aspects of civil law. In consultation are Robert Fine (seated) and partners (from left) Dan Kohane, Lawrence Franco and Ann Evanko.
Photographed by Nina Barnett in Buffalo, NY

Right: "The challenge of trying to solve different problems is what makes law interesting," says Bob Feldman, a partner at Gross, Shuman, Brizdle & Gilfillan in Buffalo. Feldman believes that Jewish tradition predisposes many Jews to the legal profession. "There's a Talmudic history," he says, "that honors the kind of debate and discussion that goes into law."
Photographed by Nina Barnett in Buffalo, NY

Left: Brothers on the Hill. U.S. Senator Carl Levin of Michigan and U.S. Representative Sandy Levin of Michigan's 17th District confer in the marble halls of the Russell Senate Office Building. Sons of Detroit attorney Saul Levin, Carl, 54, and Sandy, 57, are both Democrats who've worked together on unemployment benefits, arms control, government contract reform, expanded Social Security services ... and their squash game.
Photographed by Nick Kelsh in Washington, D.C.

Above: Suburban New Yorkers rotate into a pick-up game of basketball at the Sid Jacobson-North Shore Young Men's and Young Women's Hebrew Association, a brand-new, $12 million facility in East Hills, Long Island. These sometime-jocks play twice a week through the winter until softball season sends them outside in the spring. Andy Tanen, 39, (with towel) is a manufacturers' rep working in the pipe, valve and fittings industry. He says the competition is tough ... even when they manage to keep the speedy high-school kids off the court.
Photographed by Peter Essick in East Hills, NY

Above: Born in Wichita, Kansas, Alan Greenberg calls the shots from behind his desk on the trading floor of Bear, Stearns & Company, a Fortune 500 investment banking and brokerage firm. Greenberg—known as "Ace" by friends and colleagues—joined the firm in 1949 and was made CEO in 1978.
Photographed by David Burnett in New York City, NY

Right: "I've invented dozens of dollar-bill effects," says Mike Bornstein, a magician for more than 50 years. "I've written three books just on dollar bills." During the week, Jewish magicians gather at Cafe Edison off Times Square in Manhattan to eat, gossip and trade tricks. Mike's cronies include (from left) George Kaplan and Marvin Steiner.
Photographed by Nina Barnett in New York City, NY

Left: Jeff Hoffman, 44, went into the family business: outer space. His father, Burton Hoffman, was an astronomer. With a doctorate in astrophysics from Harvard, Jeff decided to take things a bit further and became an astronaut. "My mother," Jeff says, "might have preferred that I become a doctor. She worries."

As a member of the fourth Discovery space shuttle mission, Hoffman was in orbit for seven days in 1985. (He packed a *mezuzah* and *tallit*.) "Sleeping in space was an absolute delight," he says. "You don't need a bed. You strap yourself down just enough so you won't bump into anything and then close your eyes." Here Jeff is shown in a training module that simulates private sleeping quarters aboard the shuttle.

Photographed by Shelly Katz in Houston, TX

Above: In 1904, at age 8, Nathan Birnbaum sang for pennies in the PeeWee Quartet on New York's Lower East Side. Today, George Burns, one of America's best-loved entertainers, looks forward to 1996, when he plans to celebrate his 100th birthday with a two-week booking at the London Palladium.

Photographed by Douglas Kirkland in Beverly Hills, CA

Above: "The job is its own reward," says Judith Plotz (left), a 24-year veteran of George Washington University's English department. Born in Brooklyn and educated at Harvard, Plotz teaches everything from freshman literature to graduate courses. Freshmen Jonathan Lipton (center) and Marci Safran (right) discuss some points raised during "The Rhetoric of Television," a class Plotz is teaching for the first time in her career. **Photographed by Nicholas H. Sebastian in Washington, D.C.**

… I discovered that I should write about my environment, which means the Jewish people, the Yiddish-speaking people.—I.B. Singer

Above: Although author Isaac Bashevis Singer immigrated to America in 1935, his heart and dreams remain in the vanished world of Eastern European Jewry. His fantastic tales, written in Yiddish then translated into 16 languages, are filled with ghosts, *yeshiva* boys and odd characters at once foolish, heroic and touching. Singer has written more than 30 books, and in 1978 he won the Nobel Prize in literature.
Photographed by Susan Greenwood in Surfside, FL

Below: The first lines of one of the oldest books in the world glow on a typesetting monitor at Mesorah Publications Ltd. in Brooklyn. Rabbi Nosson Scherman, editor in chief, reviews the text for a Hebrew language Bible to be distributed worldwide. Each year, American publishers produce between 500 and 700 volumes in Hebrew.
Photographed by Bill Ballenberg in Brooklyn, NY

Left: "For me, the edge of space has always been a beckoning kind of thing," says Dr. Richard Green, explaining a fascination with astronomy that began in childhood. Using the Schmidt and other telescopes at Kitt Peak National Observatory in Arizona, Green studies quasars, stellar remnants and distant galaxies in an attempt to understand the origin of the universe. "When it comes to dealing with issues like the creation of the universe," says Green, a committed Conservative Jew, "you bring to it something beyond cold logic. You assume an underlying order."
Photographed by Jim Richardson at Kitt Peak, AZ

Above: The origin, discoveries and implications of genetic engineering are the focus of a monograph by Drs. Paul Berg and Maxine Singer. Berg, the Willson Professor of Biochemistry at Stanford University Medical Center, was the recipient of the 1980 Nobel Prize in chemistry for his study of the biochemistry of nucleic acids, the building blocks of DNA. Singer's qualifications are equally impressive—she is acting president of the Carnegie Institution of Washington, a research foundation devoted to the advancement of study in the physical and biological sciences.
Photographed by Doug Menuez in Palo Alto, CA

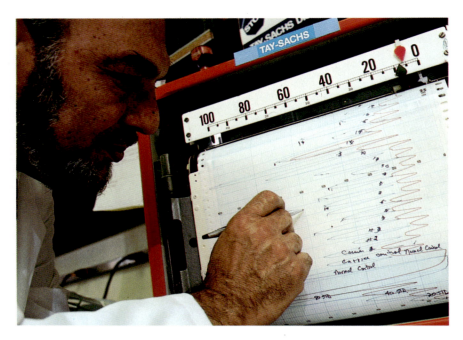

Above: Dr. Paul Tocci, the director of biochemical genetics at the University of Miami, has researched Tay-Sachs disease since 1960, when it was the subject of his doctoral dissertation. Once confined to the Jewish population alone, Tay-Sachs, a disease which gradually causes deterioration of the central nervous system, is now found among non-Jews as well. In addition to testing patients, Tocci, who is not Jewish, devotes a lot of time to educating the Jewish community. "I might as well be Jewish," he says, "I've spoken at more temples than most rabbis."
Photographed by J.B. Diederich in Miami, FL

Right: Surgeon in chief A. Gerson Greenburg just finished assisting a younger surgeon on a three-and-a-half-hour portacaval decompression at Miriam Hospital in Providence, Rhode Island. Organized in 1926 as a place where Jewish doctors could practice, Miriam is now affiliated with the Brown University Program in Medicine. "After direct patient care," Greenburg says, "the biggest thrill of being an academic physician is teaching a resident to do what I do—doing it right."
Photographed by Bill Ballenberg in Providence, RI

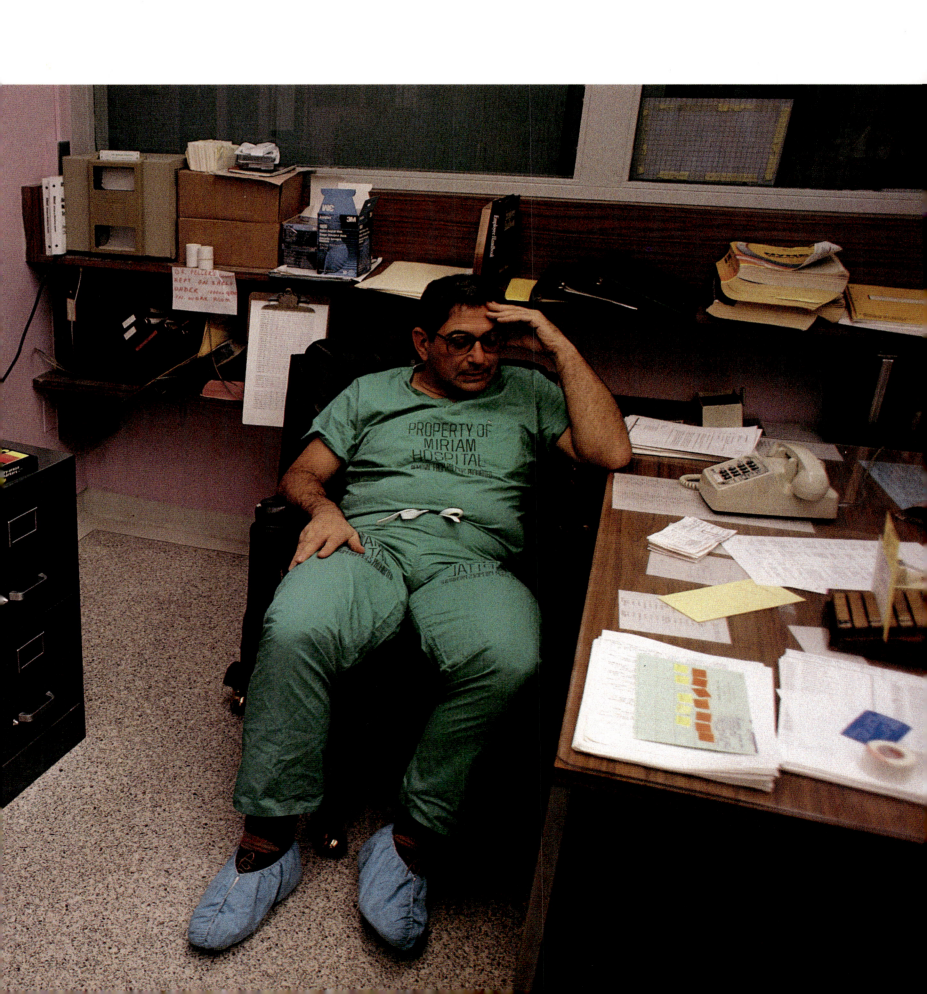

Here in Patten, Maine, where my family and I are the only Jews, I was accepted initially as a physician, and my religion was simply overlooked. After 11 years, that has changed. My patients offer *Hanukkah* greetings or holiday greetings, instead of the ubiquitous 'Merry Christmas.' At our clinic party last year, the staff presented me with a brass *menorah* from the Hammacher Schlemmer catalogue. They said they wanted to reciprocate for the years I had acknowledged their traditions. I was very touched."

Dr. Ron Blum (seated at right) and his family live in the farthest reaches of northern Maine's timber country, 35 miles from the nearest hospital. He moved to Maine in 1975, when he could no longer tolerate what he calls "the urban pollutions" of New York City. Since then, he has become an old-fashioned country doctor. Housecalls are routine, and a knock at the door transforms his dining room into an emergency room.

Two years ago, the Blum family's celebration of *Purim* was interrupted by a knock at the door. A local girl had put her arm through a pane of glass. After Blum stitched up the wound, she and her brother joined the family for the reading of the *megillah* (a scroll containing the Book of Esther) and the celebration that followed.

As occupational medical consultant for Great Northern Paper Company and other local mills, Blum spends a lot of time doctoring millworkers and anticipating potential accidents. In his spare time, he's the *mohel* for Congregation Beth El, 100 miles away in Bangor, Maine.

Dr. Blum was photographed by Richard Marshall in Sherman Station and Island Falls, ME

Right: At his office in Island Falls, Maine (population 1,000), Blum examines Kenneth Lane for strep throat.

Below: Blum treats Jewell Robinson's ingrown toenail in Robinson's kitchen. Since suffering a stroke two years ago, the former head machinist at a local lumber mill can no longer perform the simple household chores that kept him busy in retirement. "It's basically killing him not to be physically active anymore," Blum says.

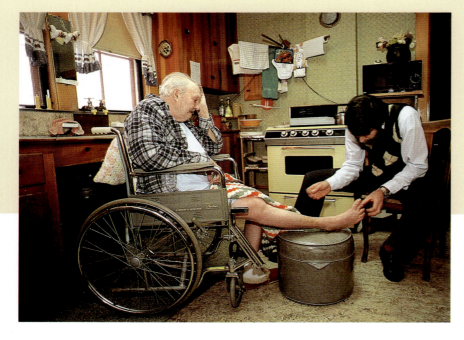

Above and preceding page: On a ranch in Petaluma, California, cowboy Scott Gerber and his dog, Annie, spend their days taking care of the cattle. Scott's chores include calving, doctoring sick stock, fencing, moving the animals from pasture to pasture and shoeing his string of horses.

Although he was raised Jewish on a chicken farm and says he feels Jewish, Scott says he is not very religious. On occasion, he'll sing some of the Yiddish folk songs he learned from his mother and grandmother. "I like the songs and want to help keep them alive," he says.

Photographed by Genaro Molina in Petaluma, CA

Right: Norbert Jakobs' family has worked in the cattle business for generations, first in Europe and now, beginning with Norbert and his brothers, in America. Jakobs Brothers Farms in Sterling, Illinois, raises 6,000 beef cattle a year. When his 4-year-old grandson, Nick, comes around, Norbert does double duty, over-seeing cattle and child. "You bet we watch him!" says Norbert. "He has no fear of cows. We have to grab him and hang on."

Photographed by Richard Marshall in Sterling, IL

Right: Zev Kron works as a diamond cutter on weekdays and as a *cantor* on *Shabbat*. Family heritage brought him to both: His father is a *cantor*, and his four uncles work as cutters and brokers. Zev spends his days in Manhattan's Diamond District making "eight counts" (cutting four-facet diamonds into eight-facet stones). Zev feels some additional pressure when cutting large, expensive stones, but not much. "There are so many things to concentrate on with any stone," he says, "so I just concentrate on doing my job right."

Below: Kron's boss, William Goldberg cuts diamonds so poorly that he was fired from his first job. Nevertheless, he kept his passion for finely cut gems and found his metier in merchandising. Goldberg's motto: "The magic is in the make."
Photographed by Nina Barnett in New York City, NY

123

Erica Kaufman of the Jewish-German Dance Theater photographed by Nick Kelsh in Philadelphia, PA

Painter Bon Gordon photographed by Nicole Bengiveno in East Machias, ME

Klezmer musician David Brody photographed by Bill Greene in Cambridge, MA

Artist Michael David photographed by Nick Kelsh in New York City, NY

Left: Almost every congregation has its sisterhood. The members attend lectures and cultural events, perform charity work and raise funds for the synagogue. At Beth Sholom Congregation in Elkins Park, Pennsylvania, sisterhood members enjoy a concert they sponsored in the sanctuary they built.
Photographed by Nick Kelsh in Elkins Park, PA

Above: More than 1400 volunteers turned out at the head-quarters of the United Jewish Appeal-Federation for "Super Sunday," a one-day telethon fundraiser. In the Big Apple alone, callers raised over $4.1 million from 23,313 donors. The UJA-Federation of New York is the largest local philanthropic organization in the world. It is a major source of private funding for social services in Israel, 130 agencies in the New York area and Jewish community needs in 33 countries.
Photographed by Jerry Valente in New York City, NY

Abraham Twerski wears a long beard, frock coat and *yarmulke*—the trappings of *Hassidism*. He goes to *shul* every morning and leads *Talmud* study. But by 8:45 a.m., every day except *Shabbat*, Abraham Twerski, the *Hassidic* rabbi, becomes Abraham Twerski, counselor to drug addicts and alcoholics. Twerski is founder and medical director of Gateway Rehabilitation Center, a residential treatment program in Aliquippa, Pennsylvania.

A ninth-generation descendant of the Baal Shem Tov, founder of *Hassidism*, Twerski originally followed the family path and entered the rabbinate. He discovered that people today often turn to psychotherapists for help, and rabbis for ceremonial officiation. "I didn't want to be a performer," he says. "I wanted to be what my father was, one of the best intuitive counselors I've ever known." So Twerski got his medical degree, his psychiatric specialty, and started treating substance abusers.

Twerski empathizes with those who succumb to chemical dependency, although he himself only drinks when blessing wine on *Shabbat*. "I see in myself personality traits of an alcoholic," he maintains. "I'm a procrastinator. I crave instant relief. I like the easy way out. I don't take the easy way out, but I have the tendency."

Known as Abe, Abey or Dr. T., Twerski enjoys the trust and affection of the people he treats. Former patients greet him with hugs or lingering handshakes at Alcoholics Anonymous meetings. In short, the rabbi has found his congregation.

Rabbi Abraham Twerski was photographed by Randy Olson in Aliquippa, PA

Left: "I've become impressed with people's blindness to their own assets," says Twerski, here holding an impromptu counseling session in Gateway's cafeteria.

Below: The doctor-rabbi mixes easily with patients at Gateway. Although he doesn't usually have time for Ping-Pong, Twerski frequently stops to talk with patients about their problems, no matter how far behind schedule he is. At the same time, however, he maintains a certain personal detachment. Says one colleague, "I think he's very much in touch with the real world, but he chooses to keep his personal self apart."

Left: About 2,000 Jews currently serve time in America's prisons. Most Jewish criminals commit white-collar crimes, but a handful are hard-core offenders. Rabbi David Maharam ministers to Stan Rosenthal and nine other Jewish inmates at the maximum-security penitentiary in Graterford, Pennsylvania. "I treat them no differently than I do my congregation on the outside," says Maharam. "I serve a group of Jews who require an educational and spiritual connection to Judaism."
Photographed by Nick Kelsh in Graterford, PA

Above: Myer Margolis, 94, is a veteran of World War I and a former printer and glass cutter. Since he retired in 1960, he and Kitty, his wife of 56 years, have been living on their Social Security. Four years ago, Myer developed Alzheimer's disease and now requires constant care, but Kitty, 84, refuses to send him to a nursing home. "It's a very hard life, and I get very little help," Kitty says, "but I can't leave him alone. I can't send him away." Fortunately, Myer and Kitty are able to live in an ocean-view apartment provided by the Jewish Association for Services for the Aged (JASA). Called the Scheuer House of Brighton Beach, this senior-citizens building houses 151 families (not all Jewish) who, because of income and health, qualify for a full range of support services provided by JASA.
Photographed by April Saul in Brooklyn, NY

Right: Single mothers, recent high-school graduates and Soviet emigrés, among others, will benefit from Diana Strauss's twirl down this makeshift, fashion-show runway in a private home in San Francisco. The 145,000 members of Women's American ORT (Organization for Rehabilitation through Training) raise funds to support career education. A worldwide ORT network operates more than 700 schools and programs in 32 countries. About 200,000 students learn skills ranging from carpentry and road maintenance to televison production, computer programming, robotics, accounting and hotel management.
Photographed by Ed Kashi in San Francisco, CA

Below: Project EZRA, a grassroots organization, puts volunteers together with the hungry and the homeless—with very little bureaucracy in between. At Tompkins Square Park in New York, Jonathan Lipnick and Misha Avramoff hand out donated juice and food to one of Manhattan's marginal survivors.
Photographed by Diego Goldberg in New York City, NY

Left: Michele Diamond, Laurie McRitchie and Joel Feldman are cleaning up Red Rock Canyon to prepare for their *Bar* and *Bat Mitzvah* celebrations. At Congregation Ner Tamid in Las Vegas, each seventh-grader in the *B'nai Mitzvah* class is responsible for performing a good deed for the community at large. The trip to Red Rock wasn't all work, though. A picnic and some rock climbing finished the day.
Photographed by Rick Rickman in Red Rock Canyon, NV

Below: Once a month, teen-agers from Congregation B'nai Amoona's youth program visit Grace Hill Settlement House in St. Louis to play with homeless children. Mike Marwit, the program's president, says that social service originates in the Jewish concept of *tikkun olam*, or repairing the world. "It starts in your own community. It's a joy to work with the children. To see them smiling and laughing and playing ... you know you've done what you came to do."
Photographed by Patrick Tehan in St. Louis, MO

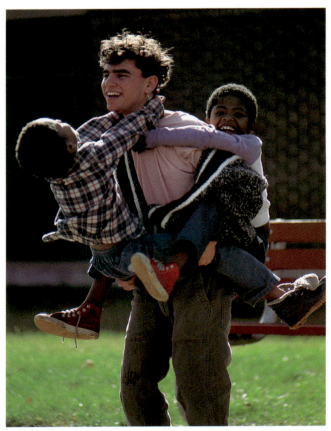

Left and above: The tiny Hebrew Benevolence Society cemetery in Columbus, Texas, had suffered 50 years of neglect. Sandwiched between an old white Christian cemetery and an old black Christian cemetery, the 117-year-old Jewish resting place looked like a little forest inside an ornate wrought-iron fence. That is, until the cemetery was adopted by Boy Scout Troop 806 of Houston's Temple Beth Israel. The troop spent more than 60 boy-hours clearing away 18 trailer-loads of debris, polishing the cemetery's gravestones, and sanding and painting the wrought iron. A local Burger King delivered free lunches to the hard-working Scouts, and the mayor of Columbus (population 4,000) promised that the town would maintain the cemetery once the young men had spruced it up.

Photographed by Skeeter Hagler in Columbus, TX

How precious is Thy loving-kindness, O God! And the children of men take refuge in the shadow of Thy wings ... For with Thee is the fountain of life; in Thy light do we see light.—Psalms: 36:8-10

Above: In 165 B.C.E., Judah Maccabee and his guerrilla army routed the Syrian-Greek occupiers from ancient Palestine and rededicated the Temple in Jerusalem. Legend has it that the Maccabees could find only a day's worth of untainted holy oil for the Temple's eternal *menorah*. The oil, however, burned for eight days. Thus, the miracle of *Hanukkah*, the Festival of Lights. Rabbi Daniel Polish explains *Hanukkah*'s meaning to (from left) Sam Karp, Sara Mandelbaum, Erin Wolson and Dara Haenel, kindergartners at Temple Beth El.
Photographed by William DeKay in Birmingham, MI

Right: *Hanukkah menorahs* keep finding their way into the Rosens' Seattle-area home—a gift or two, a couple of clay *menorahs* the kids made in Jewish day school, a small one bought for travel. In all, the Rosens own 15 *menorahs*. Here, Stanley and Michele, 11-year-old Mimi and 6-year-old Jack pitch in to light candles. "Sometimes we have little fires we have to put out," concedes Michele, "but it's real pretty."
Photographed by Peter Haley on Mercer Island, WA

Preceding page photographed by Ricardo DeAratanha in Beverly Hills, CA

Above: It takes an ambitious appetite to polish off one of Leo Steiner's towering pastrami sandwiches. Indeed, volume is one of the ingredients which has led to the immense popularity of the Carnegie Delicatessen, which serves hundreds of pounds of pastrami every day. Steiner, who ran the restaurant with partner Milton Parker for 12 years, died in late 1987.
Photographed by Michael O'Brien in New York City, NY

Right: Customers storm the counter at Canter's Delicatessen, located in the predominantly Jewish Fairfax section of Los Angeles. Miriam Bilas, Roy Buckner, Tania Shamuliou and Esther Silber handle crowd control.
Photographed by Jim Mendenhall in Los Angeles, CA

Preceding page: "Sammy's is a family place," says Stan Zimmerman, owner of Sammy's Famous Roumanian Restaurant on Manhattan's Lower East Side. "You can sit with three or four generations at the same table."

   Sammy's specializes in Eastern European Jewish delicacies, from chopped liver with onions fried in *schmaltz* (chicken fat) to jellied calves feet. High-octane garlic is added to nearly every dish. Zimmerman makes sure his patrons leave satisfied as well as smelly. "You roll out of here," he says. "It's like a *Bar Mitzvah* dinner every night, without having to give a gift."
Photographed by Jerry Valente in New York City, NY

Left: Bernard Mendlovits is one of 20 rabbis employed by the Alle meat-processing plant in Brooklyn. Bernard serves as a *shohet*, or ritual slaughterer. Not permitted to hunt or kill, Jews appoint a *shohet*, who, by virtue of his dedication, will not become brutalized by his calling. *Kosher* laws require that animals be slaughtered as painlessly as possible, and that the meat be drained, soaked and salted so that most of the blood is removed. Jews believe that an animal's blood is its life and soul and hence not for human consumption.
Photographed by Bill Ballenberg in Brooklyn, NY

Below: It's too big to be called the quintessential deli, and it's not *kosher* so it can't be called a purist's deli. But even in New York, Katz's is, by far, the grandest deli—the Grand Central Station of delis, where the whole world comes to taste secret-recipe hot dogs and salamis. Katz's ancient slogan: "Send a salami to your boy in the army."
Photographed by Jerry Valente in New York City, NY

Above: Fish-eye view. Smoked white fish entice a shopper at Russ & Daughters Delicatessen on Houston Street in lower Manhattan.
Photographed by Steve Krongard in New York City, NY

Right: At Scotty's Delicatessen on the Lower East Side, there are no fixed prices ... if you know how to bargain.
Photographed by Bill Aron in New York City, NY

Blessed art thou, O Lord our God, King of the Universe, who created the fruit of the vine —from the *Kiddush*, the blessing over wine.

Above: Royal Kedem Winery produces more *kosher* wine than any other winery in America—up to two million gallons annually. The Herzog family founded Kedem eight generations ago in Czechoslovakia, then transplanted it to New York after the Communist government expropriated the land in 1948.

At right, Kedem treasurer and family member Joseph Stern inspects grapes on the 180-acre vineyard. During harvest, called the "crush," all of the winery's workers, white-collar included, pick grapes.

Photographed by Bradley Clift in Marlboro, NY

Left and below: *Matzoh*, or unleavened bread, reminds Jews of their hasty escape from ancient Egypt and slavery. "And the people took their dough before it was leavened ..." —Exodus 12:34. Traditionally, Jews commemorate the Exodus by eating *matzoh* during the week of Passover, but Jews and non-Jews alike eat millions of the crackly wafers every week.

Sol Friedman took a summer job at the B. Manischewitz Company *matzoh* bakery in Jersey City 20 years ago. Now he's plant manager, responsible for about half the *matzoh* production in the United States. Sol's job involves a degree of precision. *Matzoh* must be fully baked in less than 18 minutes to avoid inadvertent leavening. The quality-control team at Manischewitz bakery also includes Rose Berlin, below, who checks the packaging before shipment.
Photographed by Steve Krongard in Jersey City, NJ

Left and below: Panacea or placebo? Chicken soup has been called the Jewish penicillin, a folk remedy and just an old wives' tale. As far back as the 12th century, Maimonides himself called it a medication. A more contemporary rabbi says it represents "the love, compassion and devotion of the Jewish mother."

Pulmonary physicians at Mount Sinai Medical Center in Miami, Florida, decided to settle the question once and for all. Their scientific inquiries determined that the vapors from chicken soup temporarily "help increase nasal mucous velocity," thereby speeding infectious agents out of the respiratory system. Score one for tradition.

At 9:00 a.m. on a Sunday in November, the six finalists in the Best Chicken Soup Cook-Off entered the kitchens of the Hotel Sofitel in suburban Minneapolis and lit their gas burners. They sectioned and skinned the chickens, then threw vegetables, spices and bouillon into pots. For five hours, the soups boiled and simmered. Discerning noses compared vapors. Practiced palates measured flavors. At the afternoon awards ceremony, below, the panel of judges scored the soups in four categories (taste, appearance, aroma and originality) and announced their winner: Phil Steinberg (center, in photo at left) whose soup evolved from his mother's recipe. "Fortunately, my mother's secret ingredient was love, not fat," Steinberg said.

Photographed by Joe Rossi in Bloomington, MN

The *Mashgiah*: the white-hot flame (2,200 degrees Fahrenheit) of Rabbi Moshe Heisler's blowtorch burns out any food residue that might be imbedded in the walls of an all-purpose tilt-fryer in the kitchens of Denver's Marriott City Center Hotel. This process called *libun* (literally whitening), or *kosherizing*, is required by the dietary laws to purify non-*kosher* cooking utensils and surfaces and make them suitable for *kosher* food preparation. The Marriott calls on Heisler whenever the hotel hosts occasions requiring *kosher* meals; in this case, it's a fundraising dinner for Israel Bonds.

Heisler is the only full-time *mashgiah* (*kosher* supervisor) in Denver, a position he has held since 1977. Employed by *Vaad Hakashrus*, a communal *kashrut* supervision group, Heisler keeps very long hours, inspecting and *kosherizing* everything from food-processing plants (e.g., Oroweat Bakeries, the Bagel Store, Safeway Dairies, Arctic Pacific Fisheries) to restaurants, banquet halls and private homes. *Vaad Hakashrus* is very picky; their clients must meet the standards outlined in the *Code of Jewish Law* before a *mashgiah* will certify the facility. Certification allows the manufacturer or vendor to label their products *kosher*.

Photographed by Jay Dickman in Denver, CO

Left: Every Friday morning, Rabbi Pinchas Weberman inspects and repairs the *eruv* (boundary) he has pieced together around the 10-mile perimeter of Miami Beach. Jewish law severely restricts activities like carrying and lifting outside the household on *Shabbat*, but tradition created the *eruv hatserot* (mixing of courtyards) as a legal fiction to get around the practical problems caused by the law.

The *eruv* is a physical line which enlarges the boundaries of each household to encompass whole neighborhoods, thus converting the entire community into a single home or courtyard. Provided the *eruv* is built and maintained by people skilled in the art (*eruv* boundaries often use telephone pole lines, fences, building walls, etc.), observant Jews can spend the Sabbath day visiting friends on foot, pushing baby carriages and carrying prayer books and keys within its limits. Jerusalem's thirty-mile *eruv* is thought to be the world's largest.

Photographed by Debra Lex in Miami Beach, FL

Above: The *mikvah*. Seven days after the end of her menstrual period, following a thorough scrubbing and bath, a woman enters a community *mikvah* in the Crown Heights section of Brooklyn. After immersion and a benediction, she will be free to resume marital relations, suspended nearly two weeks before at the onset of her period.

The *mikvah* ritual is strictly observed by Orthodox women and occasionally by men. Through the centuries, this monthly rite of sexual abstinence and self-purification has been a key component of the *taharot hamishpacah* (laws of family purity). Its observance is so important to Orthodox Jews that the community is required to sell a *Torah* scroll, if necessary, in order to pay for the construction of a *mikvah*.

Photographed by Donna Ferrato in Brooklyn, NY

Above: Pearl Krasnjansky and her 2-year-old daughter, Sarah, utilize the world's biggest *mikvah*—the Pacific Ocean. Dietary laws require that new dishes be immersed in a moving body of natural water for purification. Usually a special bath is built by the community for this purpose. But, where there's no bath, it's back to the original.
Photographed by Joy Wolf in Honolulu, HI

Six days shalt thou labor, and do all thy work; but the seventh day is a sabbath unto the Lord thy God ...—Exodus 20:9-10

Above: According to the *Torah*, *Shabbat* is the most important Jewish holiday. It is also the loveliest.

"Just before lighting the candles, I empty my mind of everything that isn't *Shabbat*," says Moroccan-born Deanna Pool. "I am filled with immense joy ... the warmth and glow of the candles, the joy of welcoming *Shabbat*. I prepare for it all week long. I bake my own *hallah* and do all the cooking. When *Shabbat* comes, I am totally free from secular life. It is a day of complete and total devotion to God. I feel a glow that remains with me for two or three days after."
Photographed by Dan White in Lees Summit, MO

Right: Lighting candles to begin *Shabbat* is among the few *mitzvot* (commandments) reserved for females. Six-year-old Elisabeth Kostin does the honors this *Shabbat*.
Photographed by Bradley Clift in West Hartford, CT

Above and right: Most of the original members of San Francisco's Temple Emanu-El were lured west by the Gold Rush of the 1850s. Once located in the Italian North Beach district, and then downtown on Sutter Street, Emanu-El moved to its present location in the residential Richmond neighborhood after the San Francisco earthquake and fire of 1906. With more than 1,600 families, Emanu-El's membership is the largest in Northern California.
Photographed by Doug Menuez in San Francisco, CA

Above: Every Friday before sunset, some of the Jewish soldiers at Fort Jackson, South Carolina, lay down their rifles and head for synagogues in nearby Columbia. Soldiers in basic training must wear their uniforms at all times, even during prayer. From left: Barry Fay, Troy Inskeep, Hazel Dickinson and Elizabeth Evans worship at the Tree of Life Congregation.
Photographed by Joanna B. Pinneo in Columbia, SC

Right: "The kids go away to a university, get a profession and don't come back," says one older member of dwindling Congregation Shearith Israel. The congregation was founded in Wharton, Texas in 1913 to serve the many Jewish merchants and garden farmers who came to southeast Texas—some directly from Europe via Galveston. In 1956, the congregation built a beautiful new synagogue in the shape of a *Magen David* (Star of David). There were over 100 children in the Sunday school then; today, there are only six.

Still, about 70 families, some of them traveling 50 miles, attend services held at the synagogue every other week. The synagogue can no longer afford its own rabbi, so Rabbi Aaron Weinberg of Austin drives in to conduct services.
Photographed by Skeeter Hagler in Wharton, TX

Preceding page: Friday night at Plum Street Temple in Cincinnati. The Gothic temple, with its glittering overlay of Moorish figurations, is an early monument (built in 1866) of Reform Judaism in America. The German-born rabbi who led the congregation during its construction, Isaac Mayer Wise, also established several of Reform Judaism's central institutions, including the Union of American Hebrew Congregations, Hebrew Union College, and the Central Conference of American Rabbis. Wise's energy had the effect of making the Plum Street Temple—and Cincinnati—one of the cradles of the Reform movement in America.
Photographed by Randy Olson in Cincinnati, OH

Left: Twelve-year-old Zevi Roness *davens* (prays) from a *siddur* during prayers at Oholei Torah, the *Lubavitcher* school he attends in the Crown Heights section of Brooklyn. During the day, Zevi studies *Gemara* (the *Talmud*), *Humash* (the five Books of Moses) and the *Nevi'im* (Prophets)—all written in Hebrew or Aramaic, but explained and taught in Yiddish. "No English," Zevi says, "just Jewish."
Photographed by Jerry Valente in Brooklyn, NY

Above: The chapel at Bellefaire Jewish Children's Bureau for emotionally disturbed youth offers one resident a moment's respite. Originally a home for Jewish orphans of the Civil War, Bellefaire, located in suburban Cleveland, now takes in more Christians than Jews.
Photographed by Randy Olson in Cleveland, OH

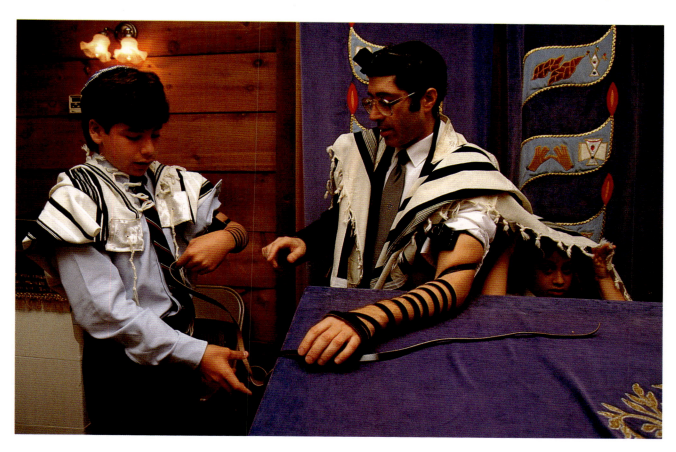

Left: *Mehitsah.* Women are separated from men during services at the Orthodox Lake Park Synagogue in Milwaukee, Wisconsin. The law can be traced to the *Gemara* (the second section of the *Talmud*), which argues that the *mehitsah*, or partition, is necessary to keep worshipers' minds on spiritual matters. This law is opposed with vigor by Jewish feminists who claim that the practice is not mandated in the Bible.
Photographed by Nick Kelsh in Milwaukee, WI

Above: *Tefillin.* At the Orthodox Torah Center of Kendall, Rabbi Hershel Becker teaches *Bar Mitzvah* trainee David Zimmerman about *tefillin*, the wearing of "signs" as commanded in the *Torah*. Tiny scrolls containing the *Shema* and other verses from Deuteronomy are put into small leather boxes which are attached to the arm and forehead by leather straps. Called *tefillin* or phylacteries, they are usually worn by men during weekday morning prayers.

"The boys are very proud to put on *tefillin*," says Becker. "It identifies them as adults and full-fledged members of the community." Seven-year-old Avraham Yaakov Becker peeks out from under his father's *tallit*.
Photographed by Debra Lex in Miami, FL

Right: No one knows for sure how many black Jews live in America, but one estimate places the number at 40,000. Some blacks are born Jewish, others convert, while others simply adopt Jewish practices. Rabbi Abihu Reuben, whose Chicago home doubles as the sanctuary for the 25-member Beth Shalom Ethiopian Hebrew Congregation, traces his Judaism to Ethiopian parents.

From ancient days until modern times, Ethiopian Jews lived largely isolated from the rest of the Jewish world, and some scholars consider them the Lost Tribe of Dan. In 1984, upward of 15,000 Ethiopian Jews made international headlines when they left the famine-plagued Sahel for Israel under the auspices of Operation Moses, a rescue effort staged by Jewish organizations worldwide.
Photographed by Richard Marshall in Chicago, IL

Below: Although one of his grandfathers was a Russian Jewish immigrant, Reuben Greenberg heard very little about his Jewish ancestry while growing up in the ghettoes of Houston. It was Jewish participation in the civil-rights movement that piqued his interest. "I remember people in the civil-rights movement questioning and arguing with rabbis," Greenberg recalls. "That amazed me. That kind of independence of mind is not fostered by a lot of religions in the world." Greenberg converted at age 26. Although his wife is Baptist, she respects his choice of faith and is even a member of *Hadassah* (a Jewish women's organization). Greenberg attends services at Synagogue Emanu-El where he sits on the board of trustees and co-chairs the adult education committee.
Photographed by Seny Norasingh in Charleston, SC

Rabbi Menachem Mendel Schneerson, leader of an estimated 500,000 *Lubavitcher Hassidim*, travels to Long Island once or twice a week to visit the grave of his father-in-law, the sixth *Lubavitcher rebbe*. Otherwise, he almost never leaves Brooklyn. He is simply too busy presiding over a movement which operates hundreds of schools, seminaries, community centers and summer camps in 28 countries.

The *Lubavitcher* movement is named for the town in White Russia where it was once based, and is also known as *Chabad Hassidism*. Rooted in Jewish mysticism, *Hassidism* swept through the *shtetls* of Eastern Europe during the 18th century. *Hassidic* adherents exhibit a religious fervor largely unknown to mainstream Judaism, particularly during holiday celebrations, when they sing and dance themselves into ecstasy.

The founder of the *Lubavitch* movement, Rabbi Schneur Zalman of Liadi (1745-1812), brought a reflective dimension to *Hassidism*. He developed the philosophy called *Chabad*, which is an acronym for the Hebrew words meaning wisdom, understanding and knowledge.

Since 1940, when Rabbi Schneerson's father-in-law, Rabbi Joseph I. Schneerson, fled the Holocaust, Crown Heights in Brooklyn has claimed the title of unofficial *Chabad* capital. About 25,000 *Lubavitchers* live in Crown Heights, and whenever the 86-year-old *rebbe* appears in public, throngs gather to venerate him.

Right: At *Chabad* world headquarters, youngsters from the sect's youth movement, Army of God, clap and sing as Schneerson makes his way among them.

Photographed by Jim Estrin in Brooklyn, NY

Left: Black fedoras and frock coats set the tone for the rigorously religious life of the *Lubavitcher Hassidim*. Most Americans, and indeed most American Jews, encounter Schneerson's followers only at "*mitzvah* tanks." These converted recreational vehicles park at busy corners in large cities while crews urge passing wayward Jews to observe religious commandments. In earlier years, young *Hassidim* stood outside of Ebbets Field, a long base hit from Crown Heights, urging Jewish baseball fans to bless the *lulav* (palm frond) and *etrog* (citron), used in celebrating *Sukkot*, as they filed out of Brooklyn Dodgers games.
Photographed by Jim Estrin in Brooklyn, NY

Above: Every Sunday, Schneerson passes out dollar bills in a two-for-one giving of *tsedakah* (charity; literally righteousness or justice). Those receiving dollar bills add at least one of their own and then donate the total amount to charity. In reality, most people keep the actual bill as a memento, donating other money instead.
Photographed by Diego Goldberg in Brooklyn, NY

*P*urim: Queen Esther, herself secretly a Jew, rescued the Jews
of Persia from certain slaughter by the evil minister, Haman.
Persuaded by her cousin Mordecai to proclaim her faith to her
husband, King Ahashuerus, she saved her people and convinced the
king to hang Haman instead. This episode from the Book of Esther
(or *megillah*) inspired the festive *Purim* celebration.

The minor holiday is a favorite with kids, who get to clatter noise-
makers in synagogue whenever Haman's name is mentioned and dress
up as little Esthers, Mordecais and even little Hamans. *Purim* gave
these three *Hassidic* siblings the chance to disguise themselves as
Queen Esther, a rabbi and a bride.

Photographed by Geoffrey Hiller in Brooklyn, NY

Above: On October 30, 1988, the Soviet Jewry Task Force of the Cleveland Jewish Community Federation hosted Summit Sunday II, a rally and learning experience in Beachwood, Ohio. More than 1,000 Clevelanders attended the event, including hundreds of Sunday-school kids bused in from local synagogues. The children saw video documentaries about *refuseniks*, heard stories told by a group of Clevelanders just back from a fact-finding trip to the Soviet Union and wrote *Hanukkah* cards to Soviet Jewish families. For the adults, there was a five-mile Freedom Run, speeches, singing and music.

Cleveland's well-organized Jewish community is widely known for its cohesiveness, creativity and generosity. Community leaders attribute this tight-knit spirit, in part, to the strength of Jewish neighborhoods; 80 percent of Cleveland's 65,000 Jews live in eight contiguous suburbs.
Photographed by Randy Olson in Cleveland, OH

Right: Among the Clevelanders who traveled to the Soviet Union to meet with Jewish *refuseniks* and other Soviet Jews was Mort Frankel, a businessman from the suburb of Pepper Pike. Two things impressed Frankel: "Number one," he says, "the absolute courage of the people who become *refuseniks*. Soviet society has improved, I'm told, over what it once was, but it's still, by our standards, a terribly oppressive system. Number two, it was amazing to find a feeling of Jewish-ness among the young people we met. For most of them, the only way they know they're Jewish is that there's a mark on their identification papers, or some older relative told them they're Jewish. I think it's miraculous that they still feel Jewish without really knowing, either culturally or religiously, what Judaism is."
Photographed by Randy Olson in Cleveland, OH

And proclaim liberty throughout the land unto all the inhabitants thereof …
—Leviticus 25:10

Below: Freedom Sunday, a rally held in December 1987, was the largest Jewish
demonstration ever mounted in the nation's capital. Two hundred thousand
people traveled from all over the United States and Canada to attend. Their
message to the Soviet Union: "Let my people go."
Photographed by Craig Terkowitz in Washington, D.C.

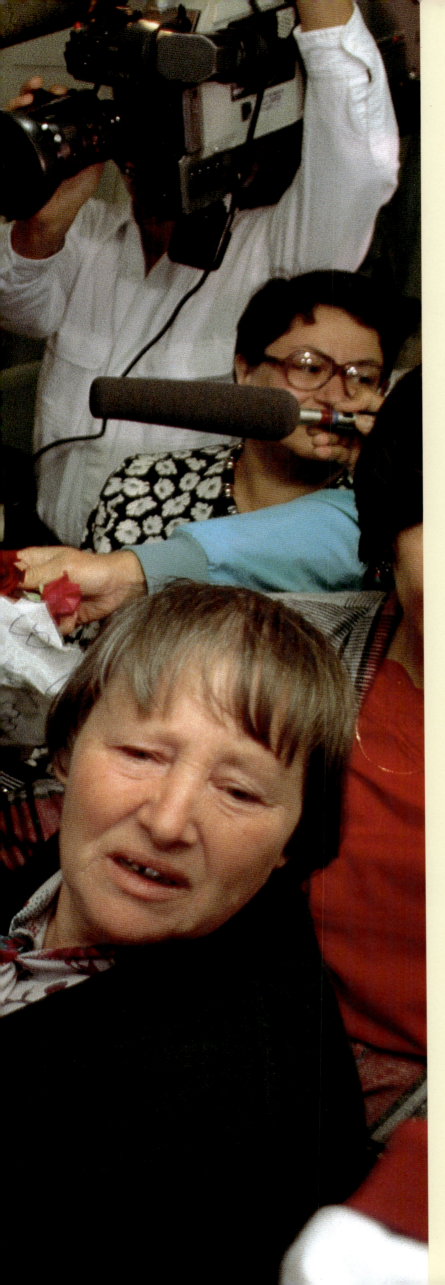

N aum Chernobelsky is arriving in his new home, Portland, Oregon, after nine years of battle with the Soviet government. *"Ya v bolshom vostorge!"* (I am overwhelmed!), he says.

At the airport, a policeman advanced through the pressing crowd toward Chernobelsky and pinned a little rose, symbol of Portland, on his lapel. "I was scared at first," Chernobelsky says. "In the Soviet Union, if a uniformed man approaches you, you only experience anxiety ... Oh! A policeman giving a rose!"

In 1979, when 51,000 Jews were allowed to leave the Soviet Union, Chernobelsky and his extended family applied to emigrate to the U.S. Within three years, most of his relatives had left to settle in Portland. Only Chernobelsky—a mechanical engineer—his wife, children and mother-in-law remained in the city of Vinnitsa in the Ukraine.

The government said that Naum would not be allowed to leave. And as additional efforts were made on his behalf, he was accused of bribery and extortion and put on trial. He and his wife were fired from their jobs.

Back in the United States, Chernobelsky's sister, Raisa Premysler, asked U.S. Representative Les AuCoin for help. She also contacted Elie Wiesel, who approached the Soviets on Naum's behalf. In fact, the entire Portland community rallied behind Raisa's efforts.

Finally, in December 1987, AuCoin argued Chernobelsky's case to Soviet officials during the Reagan-Gorbachev summit in Washington. Charges against Chernobelsky were dropped and he was released from prison. On August 7, 1988, Chernobelsky and his family departed the Soviet Union. "I believe in a bright future for my children and for us as well," Naum says. "I hope to have a job so I can support my family. For my children, they will have an opportunity to have an education in whichever field they will desire, and they will become Americans."

Photographed by Peter Haley in Portland, OR

Left and below: The debate over Israeli occupation of the West Bank and Gaza Strip has split the American Jewish community. Some feel Israel should keep the land; others say trade it for peace. The Palestinian uprising, or *intifada*, inflamed passions further as evidenced by this peace rally and counter-demonstration on Manhattan's Upper West Side.

"There was a lot of yelling and shouting," says photographer Susan Harris. "The counterdemonstrators were yelling, 'Traitors!' and the demonstrators yelled back, 'We have the right to say what we believe.' "

Photographed by Susan Harris in New York City, NY

Left: Gloria Hollander Lyon was 15 when she escaped the gas chambers at Auschwitz by jumping off a truck at the last possible moment. Separated from her family, Gloria survived six other camps before she was liberated from Ravensbrück by the Swedish Red Cross in 1945. In the months and years after the war, she discovered that nearly all of her family had also survived the Holocaust. Eventually, Gloria made her way to San Francisco where she married Carl Lyon, a lawyer who helped her bring 16 family members to America from behind the Iron Curtain. Seventeen years after the family was torn apart in 1944, Gloria, her father, brother and sister were reunited. Quoting her father, Gloria says, "You never know what sort of miracles life will present."
Photographed by Judy Griesedieck in San Francisco, CA

From the ashes and decay of the Holocaust comes the philosophy of the Jewish Defense League, an organization of Jews whose hallmark is action.—from The Principles and Philosophy of the Jewish Defense League.

Above: Irv Rubin and Avigdor Cabrera-Mueller parade the colors of the Jewish Defense League during weapons training in the Angeles National Forest. Initially formed in 1968 to patrol Jewish neighborhoods in New York City, the JDL also addresses worldwide Jewish issues in a loud and confrontational style. The most visible of the JDL's founders, Meir Kahane, now leader of the disenfranchised *Kakh* Party in Israel, is now shunned by the League for not being sufficiently militant.
Photographed by Doug Menuez in the Angeles National Forest, CA

Following page: Fifty years and 5,000 miles from *Kristallnacht*, students and teachers of B'nai B'rith Hillel at the University of Minnesota hold a remembrance service. *Kristallnacht*, the night of broken glass, shattered the thin veil of civil law that had hitherto protected Germany's Jews from violent Nazi anti-Semitism. That night, November 9, 1938, Nazi Party thugs, directed by propaganda chief Josef Goebbels, vandalized Jewish businesses and destroyed hundreds of synagogues in Germany. To many, it was the night the Holocaust began.
Photographed by Joe Rossi in Minneapolis, MN

Remember this day, in which ye came out from Egypt, out of the house of bondage; for by strength of hand the Lord brought you out from this place; there shall no leavened bread be eaten.—Exodus 13:3

Passover: The Festival of Freedom—perhaps the most widely celebrated of all the Jewish festivals—recalls the redemption of the Jewish people from 210 years of slavery in Egypt. Nine plagues were sent by God against the Egyptians. On the night of *Pesah* (Passover) the 10th plague descended: The eldest child in each Egyptian family was slain, including the Pharaoh's, while the children of the Jewish slaves were passed over. On this night, the Jews made their escape and a new nation was born in turmoil, haste and with great trust in God. To commemorate this quick departure—there wasn't even time to bake bread—Jews pause together at a Passover banquet called a *Seder*. On Nob Hill in San Francisco, Rabbi Jack Frankel and his family lift wine cups to begin their *Seder* meal.
Photographed by Roger Ressmeyer in San Francisco, CA

The hoary head is a crown of glory, if it be found in the way of righteousness. —Proverbs

Photographed by Peter Haley in Portland, OR

When a soul is sent down from heaven, it contains both male and female characteristics; the male elements enter the boy baby, the female elements enter the girl baby; and if they be worthy, God reunites them, in marriage.—from *Zohar,* the *Book of Splendor.*

Left: One such reunited soul—the Spatzes of Miami— show off their wedding portrait.
Photographed by Mary Ellen Mark in Miami, FL

Below: For High Holy Days 1988, Max and Shirley Schwitzman checked into the Crown Hotel in Miami Beach. The Schwitzmans, who live in nearby North Miami Beach, joined more than 500 other people for services in the hotel's sanctuary, and a kosher *Yom Kippur* break-fast in its large dining room. "We like going away for the holidays," says Shirley.
Photographed by Debra Lex in Miami Beach, FL

Above: After yet another severe snowstorm in their native Chicago, Mike and Kitty Zenner packed up and hit the road. They eventually ended up at Superstition Sunrise, a recreational vehicle resort in Apache Junction, Arizona. The Zenners enjoy a full life. "We ride bikes, swim, play shuffleboard—we do everything," says Kitty.
Photographed by Jim Richardson in Apache Junction, AZ

Left: In the trimming shop of C. Stoler & Company, Janet Johnson and her co-workers put the finishing touches on each casket. No nails, hardware or metal of any kind may be used in the construction of a traditional Jewish casket. Janet began working as a trimmer three years ago when the company made its move from New York City to the small town of Bristol, Tennessee. "When I first started here it was difficult because I was working with caskets. I don't think about it now, but when I see a little one it makes me sad."
Photographed by Joanna B. Pinneo in Bristol, TN

Below: At the Epstein Funeral Home, the only Orthodox funeral home in Columbus, Ohio, David Goldmeier, Joseph Nichol, Max Lowy, Bert Goldmeier, Jerry Rosen and Morris Weinstock volunteer to wash the dead and clothe them in shrouds. The *hevra kadisha*, or burial society, is known traditionally for performing *hesed shel emet* (the kindness of everlasting truth), a deed whose kindness can never be repaid.
Photographed by Randy Olson in Columbus, OH

Above and right: Sitting *shiva*, the traditional week of mourning. On November 15th, 1988, Ben Golden, a salesman and former tavern owner, died of cancer at the age of 72. That evening, Orthodox Rabbi David Stavsky came to the family's home and worked out the funeral arrangements, gently outlining the traditional ways of mourning and remembrance. Ben's sons, Ron, right, and Farrel, above, made cuts in their neckties, symbolizing the tearing away of the dead from the living. They would not shave for a week or cut their hair for a month. Mirrors in the Golden home were covered to avoid the normal vanity of life. Stavsky made sure there was a *minyan* (the minimum group of 10 men necessary for prayer) at the Golden house every day for the week of *shiva*. Friends brought in food so Rose, Ben's widow, would not have to cook.

"It was unbelievable," said 35-year-old Farrel, a schoolteacher, "There was so much support and devotion toward us. Some of the people didn't even know my father, but they were there to support us. It was a nice feeling. At the end of the day, it would get real sad, when everyone went home and I would unwind and get ready for bed and listen to my own thoughts ... my dad and I were real tight ... to know that he's not around anymore ... to know that he's gone ... the real missing of him after 35 years of always having him here. You know, he never stepped into my business, but if I ever needed him, he would never say no to me.

"All the traditions of mourning, *shiva* and everything—it lets you know that there really is a loss, not just a burial and a forgetting. It brought me closer to God, closer to my religion, closer to my people. You know, every law and tradition has a meaning to it. You can put a line to the dots and there's a picture, a full story to it. Nothing arrived out of thin air—and nothing leaves in thin air."
Photographed by Randy Olson in Columbus, OH

Following page photographed by Jerry Valente in New York City, NY

And thou shalt write them upon the door posts of thy house,
and upon thy gates.—Deuteronomy 6:9

That ye may remember and do all My commandments …

And be holy unto thy God.—Numbers 15:40

Project Photographers

Monica Almeida, *New York Daily News*
Bill Aron
Bill Ballenberg
Nina Barnett
Ernesto Bazan
Nicole Bengiveno, *New York Daily News*
Alan Berner, *Seattle Times*
Grant Black, *Windsor Star*
Torin Boyd, *Gamma Presse Images*
Michael Bryant, *Philadelphia Inquirer*
Bradley Clift, *Hartford Courant*
Ricardo DeAratanha
William DeKay, *Detroit Free Press*
Jay Dickman
J. B. Diederich, *Contact Press Images*
Michael Downey
Nancy Ellison, *Onyx*
Misha Erwitt, *New York Daily News*
Peter Essick, *City Sun*
Jim Estrin
Melissa Farlow, *Pittsburgh Press*
Donna Ferrato, *Black Star*
Paul F. Gero, *Chicago Tribune*
Diego Goldberg, *Sygma*
Bill Greene, *Boston Globe*
Lauren Greenfield
Judy Griesedieck, *San Jose Mercury News*
Skeeter Hagler
Peter Haley, *Tacoma Morning
        News Tribune*
Elaine Isaacson, *Orange County Register*
Ed Kashi
Shelly Katz, *Time*
Nick Kelsh
Douglas Kirkland, *Sygma*
Steve Krongard
Jean-Pierre Laffont, *Sygma*
Andy Levin
Debra Lex
Mary Ellen Mark
Richard Marshall, *St. Paul Pioneer
        Press and Dispatch*
Jim Mendenhall, *Los Angeles Times*
Doug Menuez
Genaro Molina, *Sacramento Bee*
Seny Norasingh
Randy Olson, *Pittsburgh Press*
Joanna B. Pinneo, *Foreign Mission Board*
Larry C. Price, *Philadelphia Inquirer*
Roger Ressmeyer
Jim Richardson
Rick Rickman, *Orange County Register*
Joe Rossi, *St. Paul Pioneer
        Press and Dispatch*
April Saul, *Philadelphia Inquirer*
Jeff Schultz
Nicholas H. Sebastian
Olga Shalygin
Patrick Tehan, *Orange County Register*
Jerry Valente
David H. Wells
Dan White
Joy Wolf, *Gamma Liaison*

Project Staff

Editor & Project Director
David Cohen

Managing Editor
Mark Rykoff

General Manager
Jennifer Erwitt

Art Director
Jennifer Barry

Chief Writer
J. Curtis Sanburn

Assignment Editors
Michael Downey
Barry Sundermeier

Production Director
Stephanie Sherman

Assistant Managing Editor
O. David Spitzler

Writer
Marshall Krantz

Design Assistant
Charles Tyrone

Production Assistants
Monica Baltz
Kathryn Yuschenkoff

Copy Editors
Jonathan A. Schwartz
Amy Wheeler

**Assistant to the
Project Director**
John Clay Stites

Picture Editors

Sandra Eisert
    San Jose Mercury News
Bill Marr
    Kelsh Marr Studios
Eric Meskauskas
    New York Daily News
George Olson
George Wedding
    Sacramento Bee

Project Consultants

Dr. Jo Milgrom
    *Center for Jewish Studies,
    Graduate Theological Union,
    Berkeley, CA*

John F. Rothmann

Rabbi Jacob Traub
    *Congregation Adath Israel,
    San Francisco*

Rabbi Sheldon Waldenberg
    Temple Isaiah, Lafayette, CA

Collins Publishers Staff

Publicity Director
Patti Richards

Sales Director
Carole Bidnick

Sponsorship Director
Cathy Quealy

Finance Director
Stanford Hays

Office Manager
Linda Lamb

Accounting Manager
Peter Smith

Senior Accountant
Jenny Collins

Sales Assistants
Brian Hajducek
Kate Kelly

Administrative Assistants
Ruth Jacobson
James Kordis
Tom LeBeau

Legal Advisors
William Coblentz
    *Coblentz, Cahen, McCabe &
        Breyer, San Francisco*
E. Gabriel Perle
    *Proskauer, Rose, Goetz &
        Mendelsohn, New York*

Dai Nippon
Printing Co., Ltd.

Ryo Chigira
Toshihiko Miyazaki
Kosuke Tago
Kikuo Mori
Mitsuo Gunji
Yoshiyasu Kosugi
Kimio Honda

This book was designed and produced entirely on an Apple Macintosh II computer equipped with a SuperMac Trinitron monitor and three DataFrame XP-60 hard-disk drives. The images were digitized with a Barneyscan and an Abaton 300. Output was generated on a Linotronic 300 printer. Project software included Aldus PageMaker, Adobe Illustrator '88, Living Videotext's MORE, and Microsoft Works. Collins Publishers has a local area network utilizing Farallon Computing's Phone-NET PLUS and THINK Technology's INBOX to link 15 Macintoshes together. We gratefully acknowledge the companies listed above for their assistance.

Photo credits:
Page 19: Photographed by
Stephen Muskie, *Wheeler Pictures*
in Bethlehem, NH

Pages 47-48: Photographed by
Nathan Benn, *Woodfin Camp &
Associates* in Brooklyn, NY

Page 104: Photographed by David
Burnett, *Contact Press Images* in New
York City, NY

Page 109: Photographed by
Susan Greenwood, *Gamma-Liaison*
in Surfside, FL

Page 193: Photographed by
Doug Menuez, *Picture Group* in the
Angeles National Forest, CA

Pages 212-13: Photographed by
Jerry Valente in New York City, NY

Pages 214-15: Photographed by
Ernesto Bazan in Brooklyn, NY

Pages 216-17: Photographed by
Michael Downey in San Francisco, CA

Pages 218-19: Photographed by
Frank Fournier, *Contact Press Images*
in New York City, NY

Page 224: Photographed by
Elaine Isaacson in Malibu, CA

Sponsor
Eastman Kodak Company

Contributors
Pan American World Airways, Inc.
Pallas Photo Labs, Inc.

Our Thanks to:
American Jewish Press Association
Atlantis Casino, Atlantic City
Beth Shalom Ethiopian Hebrew
    Congregation, Chicago
Beth Sholom Congregation, Elkins
    Park, Pennsylvania
Big Brothers & Big Sisters
    Association, Cincinnati
Charlie the Chimp & Party Art
    Productions
Children's Hospital of San Francisco
Concord Resort Hotel
Congregation B'nai Amoona, St. Louis
Congregation B'nai Shalom/Hebrew
    Association of the Deaf, Chicago
Congregation Beth Jacob, Atlanta
Congregation Emanu-El, San Francisco
Congregation Ner Tamid, Las Vegas
Congregation Rodef Shalom,
    Pittsburgh
Council of Jewish Federations
Fairmount Temple, Cleveland
Fine & Hurwitz, PC
Folkesbiene Yiddish Theatre
Fort Jackson United States Army
    Training Center
Gateway Rehabilitation Center,
    Pittsburgh
Graterford State Correctional Institute
Great Northern Paper Company
Gross, Shuman, Brizdle, & Gilfillan, PC
Isaac M. Wise Temple, Cincinnati
Jewish Community Center
    of Cleveland
Jewish Federation of Cleveland
Jewish Federation of Greater
    Los Angeles
Jewish Federation of Portland
Jewish Federation of San Francisco
Kehilla Synagogue, Berkeley
Kenneth Gordon New Orleans
Kitt Peak National Observatory
Kodalux Processing Services
Lincoln Square Synagogue,
    New York City
The Mazeltones
Miriam Hospital, Providence
Mt. Sinai Medical Center,
    New York City
Newark Beth Israel Medical Center
Resorts International, Atlantic City
Shearith Israel Congregation,
    Wharton, TX
C. Stoler and Company, Inc.
Temple Beth El, Detroit
Trump Plaza, Atlantic City
Wilshire Boulevard Temple, Los Angeles

Friends, Advisors and Consultants
Avi Abrams
Chana Abrams
Rabbi & Mrs. Sanford Akselrad
Judith Alban
David Alexander
Evelyn Alexander
Murray Alexander
Eliyahu Alpert & Family
Eric D. Altholz
Debbie Amster
Robert Aranson
Chris Araujo
Dr. Isa Aron
Robert Arrow
Jeff Atlas
Les AuCoin
Fred & Juli Austin
Misha Avramoff
Judi Ayal
Debbie Balaban
Steven Ball
Ruth Banen
Elena Baranova
Nancy Bardacke
Rabbi David Baron
Herbert Barton
Jerold Bass
Frances Batt & Family
Allen Bayer
Jeanne Bayer
Rabbi Hershel Becker
Rabbi Leonard Beerman
Reuben Beiser
George Bekeffy
Lionel Bell
Lena Benatovich
Stuart Benick
Rabbi Robert Benjamin
Warner Benjamin
Sharon Bennet
Paula Berengut
Dr. Paul Berg
Mark Berger
Lisa Berlin & Family
Rabbi Sandra Berliner
Alan Berman
Suzan Berns
Gregg Berryman
Alison Beskin Littwin
David Biale
Roger Bishop
Rabbi Sholem Blank
Elaine Blankenship
Moise Bloch
Linda Block

Roger Bloom
Paula Blum
Dr. Ronald Blum & Mary Lou Evitts
Hansey Bodinhyme
Manute Bol
Leslye Borden
Art Boyers
Theresa Bragg
Rabbi Kenneth Brander
Patti Breitman
Joel Breskin
Kay Brief
Joel Brooks
Jim Burger
Neal & Cindy Busis & Family
Dr. Sidney Busis
Richard Butler
Terry Campbell
Jacklyn Canter
Pam Canter
Julie Cantor
Barbara Caplan
Clayton Carlson
Jeff Carr
Rabbi Ari Cartun
Tom Casey
Jeffrey Cepler & Family
Ze'ev Chafets
Judy Chalmer
Dave Chambers
F. Ian Chapman
Leah Chase
Art Cherdack
Arta Christiansen
Beth Churchill-Fantz
Tom Clynes
William Coblentz
Daniel Cohen
Kara Cohen
Norman & Hannah Cohen
Sandy Cohen
Steven & Ellyn Cohen
William G. K. Cohen
Rabbi Edward Cohn
Robert Cohn
Chuck & Paula Collins
Paul Conrad
Sue Contois
Douglas Cook
Rabbi Julian Cook
Don Cooper
Lisa Correu
George Craig
Steve Curtis
J.J. Cutler
Steve Danowitz
Michael David
Paula David
Tony & Malka David
Jim Davis
Dr. & Mrs. Frank Del Muro
Jesse Del Muro
Alan & Diana Dell
Albert Demb
Ray DeMoulin

Gertie Denn & Family
Herman, Manuel & Sidney Denn
Meyer Denn
Susan Cohen DeStefano
Cynthia Dettelbach
Chickie Dioguardi
Kevin Doherty
Sheila Donnelly
Peter Drachsler
Arnold Drapkin
Gene & Gayle Driskell
Zahava Druin & Family
Steve Dry
Mike Dubridge
Ami Ducovney
Oscar Dystel
Roberta Dzubow
Lois Eagleton
Lisa Edmondson
Linda Ehrenreich
Ann Eisen
Arnold Eisen
Dr. & Mrs. Richard Eisenberg
Rabbi David Eliezrie
Rabbi David Ellenson
Jim Eller
Roberta Elliot
Rabbi Yisroel Engel
R.D. Eno
Ron Enriquez
Connie Enzminger
Jeffrey & Susan Epstein
Marjorie Epstein
Ellen Erwitt
Elliott Erwitt
Delia Escalante
Robert Eskin
Rabbi Seymour Essrog
Janice Eventoss
Michael Fanizza
Craig Farnum
Mark Federman
Craig Feiner
Stacy Feiner
Wayne Feinstein
Rabbi Yechezkel Feldberger
Bob Feldman
Rabbi Ilan Feldman & Family
Sandy Fields
Barry Fierst
Robin Fine
Dana Fineman & Family
Evie Fingerman
Eric Fischler
Brian & Marilyn Fishel
Craig Fisher
Rabbi Joshua Fishman
Dr. Kay Fishman
Kim Flasco
Deborah Ford
David Forman
Ken Fossan
Richard Frank

Rabbi Bernard Frankel
Sara Frankel
Robert Fredy
Dr. Melvin Freeman
Phillip Friedlander
Burt Friedman
James Friedman
Kinky Friedman
Lisa Friedman & Tom Mellins
Norm Friedman
Rabbi Shlomo Friedman
Rabbi Yosef Friedman
Michelle Frisch
Rabbi Elyse Frishman
Rabbi Meir Fund
Capers Funné
Helen Galen
Chaplain Stephen Gantt
Bert Garr
Anabel Garth
Howard Gelberd
Scott & Terri Gerber
Marla Gerecht
Bob & Libbie Gersten
Bill Giordano
Arnie Girnum
Rabbi Carol Glass
Jean Glasser
Scott Glassman & Family
Dr. Samuel Goetz
Amy Goldberg
Betty Goldberg
Rabbi Hillel Goldberg
Tara Goldberg
William Goldberg & Family
Dr. & Mrs. Raymond Goldblum
Reuven & Yehudit Goldfarb
Vida Goldgar
Rabbi Doug Goldhammer
Shiman Golding
Bob Goldman
The Goldmeiers
William Goldring
Adel Goldsmith
Rosa Goldstein
Samuel Goldwyn, Jr.
Phyllis Goodman
Bon Gordon
Leslie Gordon
Nancy Gordon
Rabbi Bruce Gotlieb
John Graham
Karen Grant & Family
Patrick & Mary Grant
Mr. & Mrs. William Grant
Don & Joan Green
Sherri Greenbach

Mort Greenberg
Rueben Greenberg
Dr. Gurson Greenburg
Aramalona Greenfield & Family
Barry Greenspan
Rabbi Ellen Greenspan
Dru Greenwood
Rabbi Saul Grife
Gordon Gross
Miriam Grunfeld
Chaim & Yaffa Gunner
David Hagerman & Susan Wels
Lena Hahn-Schuman & Family
Michael Hall
Alice Handelman
Lauren Hankin
Pam Harrison
Erica Hasken & Family
Terry Hastings
Steve Haugen
Harry Heineman
Laura Heller
Judy Hellman
Malcolm Helman
Tina Helsell
Barbara Herman
Otilia Hernandez
Rabbi Richard Hertz
Ernest Herzog
Mr. & Mrs. Gaston Hirsch
Rabbi Richard Hirsch
Jeff Hoffman
Nancy Hoffman
Paula Holcomb
Eugene Holt
Inez Horn
Richard Horowitz
Arthur Horwitz
Patricia Housen
Dr. & Mrs. Steven Huberman
Phyllis Hudeck
Sister Elizabeth Ann Hughes
Sheldon Hurwitz
Stanley Hurwitz
Jonathan Hyde
Bob Hyfler
Lynn Iannielo
Julanne Isaacson
Peggy Isaak
Claudia Jacobs
Louis Jacobs
Phil Jacobs
Dolf Jakobs
Manfred Jakobs
Norbert Jakobs
Brackman Joerg
Diane Johnson
Rabbi Douglas Kahn
Dr. Madelyn Kahn
Anna Kamdar
Devyani Kamdar
Mira Kamdar
P.P. Kamdar

Pravin & Caroline Kamdar
Wendy Kamenoff
Barbara Kamilar
Rabbi Lewis Kamrass
Jean Kaplow
Gina, Rafael & Sara Kapustin
The Kase Family
Troy Kashon
Gerald Kass
Michael Kassof
Beth Katz
Joe Katz
Nancy Katz
Kris Kelly
Louis Kemp
Bob Kennedy
Merle Kennedy
David Kent
Robert Kern
Betty Keva
Rabbi Khosh Kheraman
Mark & Alle Khromchenko & Family
Francoise Kirkland
Rabbi Robert Kirschner
Sandy & Judy Kivowitz
Marc Klein
Katherine Knoles
Nan Koehler
Randy & Laurie Koehler & Family
Jonathan Kollin
Eileen Kollins
Sheva Kolt & Family
Harry Kosanski
Dane & Michele Kostin & Family
Dorothy Kowaloff
The Kowaloff Family
Carol Kranitz
Rabbi Itchel Krasnjansky & Family
Dr. J. R. Krevans
Jeff Kriendler
Rabbi Yehuda Krinsky
Marvin Krislov
Anna Krivonosov
Rabbi Leah Kroll
Esther Krom
Rabbi Barry Kugel
Susan Kurlander
Dr. Joseph Kushner
Eliane Laffont
Brad Lakritz
Sonia Land
Morton Landowne
Howard Langor
Robert Lask
Gertrude Lasky
Kay Lavitt
Barbara Lazaroff
Pearl Lebovic

Rabbi Yehuda Lebovics
James Lee
Allan LeFebvre
Bob Leiter
Lisa Lenkiewicz
Jim Leonard
Nora Lester
Burton Leventhal
Richard Levick
U.S. Senator Carl Levin
U.S. Representative Sandy Levin
Jack Levine
Dr. Sandra Levine
Aaron Levinson
Mr. & Mrs. James Levinson
Ellen Levitt
Gary Levy
Leo Levy
Paula Levy
Zoya Leybin & Family
Gene Lichtenstein
Lynn Lieberman
Minna Lieberman
Molly Lieberman
Lisa Linkiewicz
Debra Lipian
Rabbi Bernard Lipnick
Jonathan Lipton
Michael Lipton
Mark Lit & Family
Pat Litt
Daveen Litwin
Mr. & Mrs. Edward Lloyd
Tom & Susan Lloyd
Richard LoPinto
Barbara Loren
Jackie Lowe
Patty Lucas
Gloria Lyon
Judi Magann
Cindi Maggied
Rabbi Arnold Magid
Rabbi Richard Maharam
Julie Mahdavi
Morris Maline
Cantor Josef Malovany
Robert Mann
Gayla Margolin
Myer & Katherine Margolis
Nancy Margolis
Dan Mariashin
Bill Markovich
Mike Marshall
Colleen Marsht
Judy Marx
Richard & Lucienne Matthews
Paul Matzger
Holloway McCandless
Randy Megibow & Family
Perrie Meltzer
Bill Messing
Carmen Michael
Susan Millberg

Rabbi Mark Miller
Michael Miller
Walter & Judy Miller
Nancy Miscia
Rabbi David Mishulovin
Steve Mittleman
Barbara Montee
Debra Mooney
Ann Moscicki
Carl Moskowitz
Charlotte Moss
Andy Muchim
Susan Musinsky
Gerald Nagel
Willy Nathanson
Jerry Neimand
Andrew Nesland
Steve Netsky
Ted & Judi Newman
Sylvia Nissenboim
Michael Novick
Rabbi Sheftel Nuberger
Michael Nutkiewicz
Howard Ogress
Amy Olson
Eleanor Olson
Carrie Padilla
Rusty Pallas
Jordan Pardes & Family
Stuart Paskow
Aaron Pearlman
Arnold & Bonnie Pearlman & Family
Roger & Carmen Pedersen
Debra Pell
Jerry Perell
Mr. & Mrs. Sholem Perl & Family
Gabe & Pat Perle
Liz Perle
Alec & Ann Petersen
Brent Peterson
Rabbi Aaron Petuchowski
Dr. Bruce Phillips
Winston Pickett
Diana Pinckley
Nancy Pitt
Minnie Planet
Tom Plaskett
Robert Pledge
Judith Plotz
Rabbi Daniel Polish
Steve Pollack
Deanna Poole & Family
Janice Popp
David Posner
Andrea Pozgay
Raisa Premysler & Family
Phil Priolo
Arthur Pulitzer

Irma Rabbino
Aron Reaven
Debby Regal
Leni Reiss
Bonnie Reiter
Martha Remenius
Bernard & Arlene Richards
Cornel & Susan Riklin
Don Robinson
Judy Rodenstein
Malcolm Rodman
Mr. & Mrs. Stanley Rosen & Family
Michael Rosenberg
Jodie Rosenbloom
Rabbi Leon Rosenblum
Stanley Rosenthal
Patti Ross
Susan Roth
Arlene Rothberg
Stewart Rothchild
Fred Rothstein
Myron Rottenstein
Razy Rottenstien
Steve Rottman
Irv Rubin
Larry Rubin
Neil Rubin
Seymour Rubin
Dr. Abraham Rudolph
Sara Grace Rykoff
Tom & Sondra Rykoff
Marci Safran
Nola Safro
Scott & Bao Sagan
Arnold Saltsman
Rabbi Murray Saltzman
Marianne Samenko
Arthur Samuelson
Steven Sands
Dr. Ira Sapan
Sharon Saslafsky
Steve Sass
Margo Savell
Rabbi Zalman Schacter
Lillian Schaechner
Brenda Schaeffer
Channa Schapiro
Rabbi Jeffrey Schein
Kalia Scheiner
Mr. & Mrs. Label Scheiner
Lionel Schlank
Bruce Schlossberg
Martin Schneider
Amy Schoenblum
Rabbi Joseph Schonwald
Rabbi Leonard Schoolman
Linda Schrack
Edith Schulman
Laura Schultz
Rabbi Myer Schwab
Rick Schwag
Eleanor Schwartz
Joan Schwartz

Dr. & Mrs. Leonard Schwartz
Rabbi Shlomo Schwartz
Thom Seaton
Rabbi Allan Secher
Shlomo & Jody Sela
Abe Shainberg
Robert Shanebrook
Ira Shapiro
Ruth Shavit
Caroline Sheffey
Steve & Danan Sherman
Dr. Gil Shevlin
Joel Shoulson
Irving Shuman
Shelly Sidlow
Julie Siepler
Joe Sigman
Cantor Paul Silbershur
Mark Silver
Ann Silverman
Ira Silverman
Dr. Maxine Singer
Phyllis Singer
Alex Smilow
Marvin & Gloria Smolan
Rick Smolan
Neal Sofman
Sheldon Sollosy
General Robert Solomon
Mark Green Solomons
Sylvia Spaisman
Rabbi Malcolm Sparer
Dick Specht
Pete Spence
Phil Sperr
Robert Spierer
John Spitzler
Ruth Spitzler
Eddie & Sheila Spizel
Pearl Stahl
Rabbi Mark Staitman
Sol Staller
Cheshire Star
Andrew & Handa Stark
Judy Stearns
Ira Steingroot
Dorothy Stern
Karen Stern
Rabbi Shira Stern
Ray Stevens
Mark Stoler
Alyson Storch
Lew Stowbunenko
Rabbi Michael Strassfeld
Peter Straus
Rabbi David Stavsky
Steve Streeter
Conrad Strohl

John & Kathy Suisman
Gary Swartz
Rabbi Michael Swartz
Mark Talisman
Nancy Tamler
Jon Tandler
Andrew & Ilene Tanen & Family
Larry Tarnoff
Christopher Taylor
Janna Thompson
Jordan Thorn
Fred Tichauer
Dr. Paul Tocci
Ella Tokar
Zalman Tornek
Richard Trank
Rabbi Moishe Traxler
Sid & Ruth Trohn
Karen Tuso
Dr. Abraham Twerski
Rabbi Michael Twerski
Irving Unger
Mario & Rebel Vaenberg
Susan Vermazen
Helen Victor Turk
Mirra Volf
Amy Wachspress
Larry Wadler & Family
Marc Wanamaker
Stuart Wax
Rabbi Don Weber
Rabbi Pinchas Weberman
Geraldine Weichman
Lehman Weichselbaum
Rabbi Joseph Weinberg
Sherri Weinblatt
Rabbi Aaron Weinburg
Rabbi Martin Weiner
Rebecca Weiner
Enita Weinstein
Stanley Weinstein
Shavey Weinstock
Mr. & Mrs. Ivan Weiss
Stephanie Whitmont
Jim Widler
Irwin Wiener
Ron Wild
Rabbi Sholem Wineberg
Sherri Winer
Simon Worrin
Jean & David Wright & Family
Lee Wunch
Steven Yaro
Lillian Yashinsky
Rita Zadoff
Sheila Zagar
Jerry Zaslaw
Rabbi Asher Zeilingold
Katherine & Myer Zenner
Steven Zerby
Sherri Ziff
Stan Zimmerman
Phyllis Zisman
Barbara Zitron
Myron Zwirn